ASSESSING HOUSING NEEDS AND POLICY ALTERNATIVES IN DEVELOPING COUNTRIES

URBAN INSTITUTE REPORT 88–4

Raymond J. Struyk

THE URBAN INSTITUTE PRESS

Washington, D.C.

October 1988

Raymond J. Struyk is Director of The Urban Institute's International Activities Center. He received his Ph.D. in economics from Washington University in St. Louis. Among his numerous publications are Housing Policy at President Reagan's Midterm (with J. Tuccillo and N. Mayer), Finance and Housing Quality in Two Developing Countries (with Margery Turner), and U.S. and West German Housing Markets (with Konrad Stahl).

Printed in the United States of America

9 8 7 6 5 4 3 2 1

Distributed by
University Press of America
4720 Boston Way
Lanham, MD 20706

Library of Congress
Cataloging in Publication
Data
Assessing housing needs and
policy alternatives in
Developing Countries.
(Urban Institute Reports; 88-
4, ISSN 0897-7399)
Bibliography p.
1. Housing policy—Developing
countries
2. Housing—Developing
countries.
3. Developing countries—
Population.
I. Title. II. Series
HD7391.S77 1988
363.5'8'091724
88-17414
ISBN 0-87766-423-4

URBAN INSTITUTE REPORTs are used to disseminate significant research findings and analysis arising out of the work of The Urban Institute. To reduce costs and minimize production delays, these reports are produced with desktop publishing technology. Like all publications of The Urban Institute Press, each Urban Institute Report is reviewed rigorously in an effort to uphold the highest standards of policy research and analysis.

The Urban Institute is a nonprofit policy research and educational organization established in Washington, D.C., in 1968. Its staff investigates the social and economic problems confronting the nation and government policies and programs designed to alleviate such problems. The Institute disseminates significant findings of its research through the publications program of its Press. The Institute has two goals for work in each of its research areas: to help shape thinking about societal problems and efforts to solve them, and to improve government decisions and performance by providing better information and analytic tools.

Through work that ranges from broad conceptual studies to administrative and technical assistance, Institute researchers contribute to the stock of knowledge available to public officials and private individuals and groups concerned with formulating and implementing more efficient and effective government policy.

Conclusions or opinions expressed in Institute publications are those of the authors and do not necessarily reflect the views of other staff members, officers or trustees of the Institute, advisory groups, or any organizations that provide financial support to the Institute.

ACKNOWLEDGMENTS

A number of people have provided invaluable help in the preparation of this report [which is based on a United States contribution to the International Year of Shelter for the Homeless]. The sponsorship of the U.S. Agency for International Development Office of Housing and Urban Programs was essential. Howard Sumka, program manager in the office, provided excellent comments on two drafts and was instrumental in obtaining a reasonable response rate to a survey conducted as part of this work.

Tammy Kang, a summer intern at the Urban Institute in 1985, is responsible for most of the calculations reported in chapters 2 and 3. Douglas Keare, Jr., an intern at the Institute in the fall of 1986, handled the computations reported in appendix B. Michele Rice provided able assistance in the analysis of the responses to our survey, the results of which are reported in chapter 4.

A final vote of gratitude goes to those people in 15 countries who responded to our survey. Conspicuous among them is the group of consultants who worked on the applications of the needs assessment model in these countries. In addition to responding to the survey, they were unfailingly cooperative in sharing the details of their work with us.

C O N T E N T S

Abstract   viii

Executive Summary   1

Are There Simple Determinants of Housing Needs?   3
What Tools are Available for Controlling
Housing Needs?   5
Impact: Policy Debate and Changes   7

1   Introduction and Overview of the Model   11

2   Housing Needs in 10 Countries   17

New and Upgraded Units   20
Housing Investment   24

3   What Drives Housing Needs?   31

Changes in Population and Urbanization   32
Housing Affordability   38
Policy Implications   43

4   Applying the Needs Model: Policy Outcomes and Lessons   49

Impact on Policy Debate and Change   50
Successful Application of the Model   55
Training   60
Overall Assessment   61

References   121

References, Country Studies   122

Appendices   65

A   Additional Information on the Assessments   67

B   Total Housing Needs in Developing Countries   83

C   Further Description of the Housing Needs Model   91

D   Questionnaire for Survey of Experience in Applying the
Model; Sample Sizes   107

TEXT TABLES

1.1 Countries to Which the Housing Needs Assessment Method
Has Been Applied   12

2.1 Summary Data on Population and Income of Countries
Studied   18

2.2 Housing Stock and Housing Needs in Selected Countries   22

2.3 Distribution of Households by Solutions They Can Afford
Using Base Case Building Standards   25

2.4 Housing Investment in the Fifth Year for Countries
Studied Under Base Case Assumptions   27

3.1 Impact of Standard Population Growth Rate on
Housing Needs   33

3.2 Impact of Increased Urbanization   37

3.3 Impact of an Increase in Share of Income Devoted to
Housing by Lower Income Households   40

3.4 Impact of Increasing Credit Availability to Reduce
Mortgage Interest Rate   41

3.5 Impact of Lower Cost Housing Solutions   42

3.6 Summary of the Impacts of Changes in Selected
Factors on Housing Needs, Investment, and Subsidies   44

4.1 Perceived Overall Benefits and Policy Changes
Associated with Applying the Housing Needs Model   52

4.2 Context of Housing Needs Assessment, in Countries
with little Apparent Effect   55

4.3 Ranking of Objectives and Audience   57

4.4 Data Inputs That Were Difficult to Assemble   59

4.5 Observations on the Value of Using the Housing
Needs Assessment Model   62

TEXT FIGURES

1   Components of Housing Needs   2

2   Determinants of Housing Investment   4

ABSTRACT

High rates of population growth and urbanization throughout the world are putting pressure on housing, pressure that will continue through the end of the century and into the next. Even so, housing needs in many countries can be met with the resources now available—if the countries adopt policies that are economically realistic and rely on individual initiative.

This report describes a model for developing such policies by determining housing needs in developing countries. It also discusses applications of the model in a set of developing countries in Africa, Latin America, and elswhere, and provides guidelines for use by shelter donor organizations, and others in the field.

Development of the Housing Needs Assessment Model was sponsored by the U.S. Agency for International Development (USAID) as a contribution to the United Nations International Year of Shelter for the Homeless (IYSH). For the past 25 years, USAID has helped developing countries establish policies to meet their housing needs. USAID shares with IYSH an understanding of the importance of reliable information about the shelter problem and the implications of adopting alternative policies.

The model is a useful tool for policy analysis. Completed applications, as reviewed in this monograph, have helped substantiate the efficacy of shelter strategies that do not rely on government subsidy. These applications show that the keys to meeting housing needs with minimal government involvement are developing appropriate, low-cost building standards and managing the economy to assure growth and adequate credit.

The housing available to most households in developing countries—especially to the very poor—is grossly inadequate. Developing countries as a group, for example, must produce an estimated 45 million additional units of minimally acceptable quality <u>each year</u> in the immediate future if they are to meet their housing needs—as estimated to cost almost 6 percent of their gross national product on average. These nations are being forced to pursue ways of dealing with their major housing problems, but their efforts are not based on a complete or realistic understanding of their housing situation or the probable impacts of different policies.

In recognition of the importance of the problems and the dire need for information; the Office of Housing and Urban Programs, U.S. Agency for International Development (USAID), sponsored development of the Housing Needs Assessment Methodology. The goal was to create a planning tool to support efforts to achieve the ambitious shelter goals of the International Year of Shelter for the Homeless (IYSH). Work on the model began in 1984 as part of the U.S. contribution to the IYSH. By the fall of 1987 the method had been applied to 15 countries and was in the process of application in 2 additional ones—a sign that it has already achieved substantial acceptance. This report is based on the experiences of 14 countries:

Barbados	Ecuador	Peru
Botswana	Honduras	Sri Lanka
Colombia	Jordan	Turkey
Costa Rica	Kenya	Zimbabwe
El Salvador	Panama	

1

The methodology produces two types of estimates that are of direct interest to policymakers: the number of new and upgraded dwelling units needed to satisfy a country's needs for acceptable housing, and the financial investment needed to produce these dwelling units.

The methodology also enables analysts to produce, and policymakers to examine, a number of alternative "policy scenarios." Since the methodology is programmed on a microcomputer, the vast number of calculations it requires can be performed quickly and accurately. Sensitivity analyses are easy to perform for policy simulations on such critical variables as interest rates and building standards. The methodology also can be used to explore the effects of different values of input data when there is uncertainty about their exact values.

The experience of applying the Housing Needs Assessment Methodology to a variety of countries indicates that the most fruitful use of the method is to assess policy alternatives. The

FIGURE 1 COMPONENTS OF HOUSING NEEDS	
Component	Determining Factors
Upgrading units	Quality of initial housing stock
New Construction: • new households • relieve overcrowding	Population, household size Extent of overcrowding at start of period

• replace nonupgradable
• replace units withdrawn
   from stock over plan period
	Quality of initial housing stock
	Durability of housing stock
	   natural disasters, etc.

iterative process of testing different ways to meet housing needs economically—for example, by lowering minimum building standards,

changing interest rate policies,   or offering housing opportunities
that induce lower   income   families   to   devote   a greater share of
their incomes   to   housing—consistently   has   led   policymakers to
consider a larger range   of possibilities than previously accepted.
The principal policy lesson, demonstrated in country after country,
is striking.   It is possible   to meet a nation's housing needs with
little or no subsidy,   if   realistic minimum building standards are
adopted.   Given the staggering   dimensions of housing needs in some
of these   countries,   this   is,   indeed,   a   central   finding.
Encouragingly,   the   results   of   the   applications   have   been
instrumental in   moving   some   of   these   countries   to   adopt such
realistic standards.

ARE THERE SIMPLE DETERMINANTS OF HOUSING NEEDS?

It would be   wonderfully   convenient   if   a   country could obtain a
rough estimate of the extent   of   its   housing needs based on other
countries' analyses   of   their   housing   needs.   For   this   to be
possible,   we   would   have   to   discover   a   basic   set   of readily
measurable factors that relate   consistently   to housing needs.   To
explore the overall   patterns   of   housing   needs, we subjected the
results   of   the   housing   needs   assessment   for   10   countries to
detailed analysis.   Although simple and accurate rules of thumb are
elusive, important points do emerge.

First, under   our   comprehensive   definition   of   housing needs,
these needs do not relate   simply   or   obviously to only one or two
demographic variables.   Rather, the outcomes are quite sensitive to
the quality of the housing   stock   at   the beginning of the period,
the definitions used to classify this stock into quality categories
(the share of the   stock   needing upgrading, etc.), the anticipated
rate at   which   units   will   be   retired   from   the   stock, and the
definition of overcrowding.

The determinants of housing investment are shown in figure 2. The relationship between the required number of units as a measure of housing need and factors which generate that need is erratic. A more consistent pattern exists, however, for the amount of investment necessary to produce the needed units. In particular, the ratio of housing investment to gross domestic product (GDP) has a fairly strong positive relationship to a country's population growth rate. To illustrate, for the 4 countries of the 10 analyzed with recent annual population growth rates of at least 3 percent, about 7 percent of GDP is invested in housing. The comparable figure for the 3 countries with population growth rates of less than 2 percent is only 4 percent.[1]

FIGURE 2   DETERMINANTS OF HOUSING INVESTMENT

Annual housing needs

Housing investment affordable by households

- income level and distribution at start of period
- real growth in household income over the period
- "mortgage terms"

Cost of minimum acceptable housing solutions

Inflation in construction costs over the period

The strength of the relationship between the population growth rate and the ratio of housing investment to GDP may seem strange in light of the lack of correlation between this growth rate and the count of new and upgraded units required to meet housing needs. The answer to this riddle is that countries with high population growth rates face the need to provide large numbers of new housing units. Countries that are growing more slowly can meet a larger portion of their housing needs through upgrading, which is a much less costly undertaking than new construction.

WHAT TOOLS ARE AVAILABLE FOR CONTROLLING HOUSING NEEDS?

Addressing the question of available tools to control housing needs involved undertaking a series of sensitivity analyses. These examined the impact on housing needs and the corresponding investment of changing key factors such as population growth rates, rate of growth of urban areas, share of income households devote to housing, mortgage interest rates, and minimum building standards selected by the country.   We   draw   several conclusions from this work.

First, it is more difficult to reduce total housing needs than the level of housing investment, as measured in the number of units of acceptable quality. The greater difficulty in reducing housing needs arises from the comparative paucity of instruments available to affect housing needs and the comparatively modest short-term quantitative effects of the instruments.   Only population, household size, and the definition of "acceptable housing" in the existing housing stock can be modified to change the number of units needed. Housing investment, however, is affected by these and a host of other factors more susceptible to short-run change than population and household size.

Second, there is no question that, over the long run, reducing population growth is a key element in reducing housing investment requirements and the subsidies that would be necessary if a government committed itself to meeting all of its country's housing needs. The analysis also suggests that reduced population growth rates will be more effective in limiting the total amount of investment necessary to meet housing needs than in reducing subsidy requirements (i.e., closing the gap between what lower income households can afford and the cost of minimum housing solutions).

Third, reduction in the required subsidies is highly responsive to three changes: lowering design standards for minimally acceptable units, reducing household mortgage interest rates through macroeconomic policy, and increasing the share of income devoted to housing by those who would receive the subsidies.

The tool most immediately at a government's disposal is lowering the minimum acceptable standards. Many countries already have adopted lower standards; but many others have considerable room for reductions, at least for "starter solutions."

Policies that increase the supply of credit for low-cost housing and reduce mortgage interest rates offer another alternative. This does not mean cutting them through subsidies or arbitrary credit restrictions, which would just replace one subsidy with another. The main target of opportunity is probably in making market-rate, formal housing loans available to lower income households which do not now have access to such funds.

Although a good deal is made of informal financial markets serving the poor, we know precious little about how the poor finance their housing. What we do know suggests that coverage is at best spotty and costs can be high compared to formal sector rates. It is also the case, in most developing countries, that increasing the supply of mortgage credit would require major changes in the housing finance system and, possibly, financial markets generally before the housing sector could compete openly for funds. On balance, reductions in mortgage interest rates offer a good deal of promise in closing the "affordability gap." Realizing this potential will, however, be a demanding task requiring years of sustained effort.

Increasing the share of income devoted to housing by those needing subsidies may be quite difficult. The key is to offer housing opportunities that are attractive enough for families to be willing to make sacrifices to occupy them. For many poor families who have lived in utter squalor, this willingness may well be present. There is, however, evidence that some sites and services projects, for example, have employed excessively high standards (and assumed too great a willingness on the part of participants to allocate income to housing), which resulted in a combination of unintended subsidies and target beneficiaries (i.e., those living in inadequate housing) not being able to remain in the project because their dwellings do not meet the standards. This experience suggests that governments must approach with great caution the idea of increasing the share of income spent on housing as a means to close the affordability gap.

IMPACT: POLICY DEBATE AND CHANGES

The Housing Needs Assessment Method is a tool for structuring policy and policy dialogue around shelter issues. The impact on national policies is a primary criterion against which to examine the success of these applications.

It is inevitably difficult to "score" the success of any study in affecting a country's policies, since so many circumstances can influence the ultimate outcomes. These conditions include the timing of presenting the results, and the degree of access to senior officials afforded to those working on the study to discuss data and present conclusions. Nevertheless, a survey of those involved in 15 of the countries included in the study offers insights into the impact of applying the model.[2]

In general, a review of the responses suggests varying degrees of effectiveness. In three countries—Barbados, Ecuador, and Zimbabwe—applying the model had a major impact. In five countries—El Salvador, Jamaica,[3] Panama, Peru, and Turkey—the application of the model seems to have had little benefit. The remaining seven countries fall somewhere in between.

Respondents commonly cited two areas of the overall benefits of applying the model, as captured in these two quotes:

• The needs method "removes the policy dialogue from one based on questionable feelings, personal biases to one predicated on a reasonably scientific basis."

● It provided "a clearer idea of the potential relationships between factors affecting housing needs investments. The base case for Jordan shows that it can manage its housing situation with some modifications in its policies and programs."

One is that the results established the size of the country's housing Problems and provided a comprehensive look at the overall housing situation. The value of such a perspective was presumably the greatest in countries where the needs estimates served as the foundation for developing a national housing strategy: Barbados, Kenya, and Jordan. In many countries, size-of-problem estimates have appeared in government documents describing the housing sector and government policy.

The other commonly cited area of results is the total housing investment and subsidy requirements necessary to meet a country's housing needs. The results generally led to discussions within government as to whether the minimum housing standards chosen were reasonable and could be achieved under expected resource constraints.

In terms of associating policy change with the results of the housing needs assessment, there is a common pattern in the three countries (Barbados, Ecuador, and Zimbabwe) where such changes were reported. In all three, the changes focused on lowering what government had defined as minimum acceptable standards in order to reduce the housing sector's total investment requirements and a consequent lowering of the subsidy amount implied by the assessment. It is worth noting that, in each case, the movement toward lower standards was led by repeated simulations with the model of alternative standards and changes in other factors; often, the issue of lowering standards was only confronted as the way to keep investment and subsidies at reasonable levels after other options had been eliminated.

The results reflected here probably represent the lower limit on the ultimate effectiveness of the needs assessment tool for housing policy. The model was applied in 1986 in several countries; hence, it is almost certainly too early for important policy changes to have materialized. More generally, in many countries, major policy changes require years of consensus building before they are accomplished--a process that may be ongoing in some of these countries. Also, the estimates may serve as a continuingly instrumental resource in the policy process. For example, housing needs estimates performed for Kenya in 1984 were used in 1986-87 in formulating a new national housing strategy.

Overall, in two out of every three countries where the model has been applied, the results have stirred some debate and assisted in governmental planning exercises. In one out of five, it had a quite immediate influence on the country's housing policies. Longer term policy effects may yet materialize in other countries. On this basis, these applications may be judged reasonably successful.

Notes, Executive Summary

1. We could not document any clear pattern between the investment ratio and the growth rate in a country's average household income level or the minimum housing standard which it defined as applicable for lower income households. Since these factors are conceptually clear determinants of housing investment (figure 2), this was somewhat surprising, but may be due to the relatively small number of countries on which the current analysis is based.

2. The applications to Brazil and the United States were not completed at the time of the survey.

3. In late 1986, the model was applied in Jamaica a second time with greater success. All references in this monograph are to the first application.

INTRODUCTION AND OVERVIEW OF THE MODEL

The poor quality of housing available to most households in developing countries—especially to the very poor—is a major problem these nations are being forced to address. Nation after nation is trying to find approaches that will yield substantial gains within a few years. Often, however, they expend these efforts without a complete and realistic understanding of the problem, leading to inappropriate solutions and "false starts" which can be extremely costly.

The first step in developing appropriate shelter strategies is to make a thorough assessment of the current needs and demand for housing, and to project how these factors are likely to change over a reasonable planning horizon—for example, 10 to 20 years. Only with clearly defined needs can a strategy to meet them be formulated and implemented.

Developing countries, as a group, must produce about 45 million additional units of minimally acceptable quality each year in the years immediately ahead if they are to meet their housing needs. A rough estimate of the corresponding annual investment is $130 billion or about 5.8 percent of their gross national product on average. Low-income countries, as defined by the World Bank, must produce two-thirds of this housing, at a cost of about $24 billion. Obviously, the needs are enormous and realistic programs for dealing with them must be developed.

In recognition of how important it is that countries understand their housing problems and the implications of alternative policies for designing national shelter strategies, the Office of Housing and Urban Programs, U.S. Agency for International Development (USAID), sponsored development of the Housing Needs Assessment Methodology. Work began on the computer model in 1984 as part of the U.S. contribution to the International Year of Shelter for the Homeless (IYSH). The goal was to create a planning tool to support efforts to achieve the ambitious shelter goals of IYSH. By the fall of 1987, the method had been applied to at least 15 countries--a sign that it already had attained substantial acceptance (table 1.1).

Table 1.1   COUNTRIES TO WHICH THE HOUSING NEEDS ASSESSMENT METHOD
           HAS BEEN APPLIED (through Fall 1987)

Barbados	Jordan
Botswana	Kenya
Colombia	Panama
Costa Rica	Peru
El Salvador	Sri Lanka
Ecuador	Turkey
Honduras	Zimbabwe
Jamaica	

Note: Applications were still underway at the time of survey in Brazil and the United States.

The Housing Needs Assessment Methodology (HNA) is a direct descendent of the well-known UN Component Method for estimating housing needs.[1]   It extends the UN method by computing the investment levels required to satisfy the housing needs that are estimated. This overview is designed to provide the reader with enough information about the workings of the model to understand

the material in later chapters.[2]   Four points about the model are
essential to such an understanding.

The first point is that the model normally employs a 20-year
planning period with results produced for each fifth year in the
period. This approach reveals the requirements for the number of
units needed in every fifth year and the related investment
requirements. The results are only for that year; they are not
cumulative 5-year totals.

The second point concerns the count of new and upgraded units
needed. Like the UN method, the model calculates housing needs as
the number of units of minimal acceptable quality required, based
on the following factors:

● formation of new households

● replacement of units already in the stock during the planning
period because they become fully depreciated or are destroyed for
various reasons

● replacement of units present in the initial year of analysis that
are rated as not economically upgradable

● construction of additional units to relieve overcrowding present
at the start of the period

● upgrading of units present at the start of the period that
required it where upgrading is economically feasible.

This is a comprehensive definition of housing needs.

The analyst (in consultation with policymakers) must provide
three key inputs for these computations:

● description of the demographic future of the country, in terms
of population growth, average household size, and the distribution
of the population among the principal regions of the country;

● classification of the initial year's housing stock into three
categories, based on unit and infrastructure attributes--
acceptable, not acceptable but upgradable, and not acceptable and
not worth upgrading;

- plan for the rate at which the housing deficits present in the initial year may be eliminated over the plan period. These deficits are the stocks of unacceptable but upgradable units, the stock of unacceptable and not upgradable units, and the number of households living in overcrowded conditions.

The model automatically requires production of a new unit for each newly formed household and replacement of any acceptable unit that leaves the active housing stock.   However, the analyst must specify the proportion of deficits present in the initial year that are eliminated over the 20-year plan period (including none or all).

These calculations (and all others in the model) are performed for up to three separate geographic areas in a country. Typically, these have been defined as metro areas, other urban areas, and rural areas. In some small countries, only an urban vs. rural definition has been used.

The third point about the model that is essential to understanding the analysis is that the calculation of the investment required to meet the number of housing units needed begins by determining the amount that households in each income quintile in each of the geographic areas can afford for housing. Affordability is then computed for 15 groups of households, based on the income level of households in a given group, the share of income they spend on housing, and the terms used to capitalize their investment.

Once affordability levels are known, the obvious next question is: what can these households actually buy?   To answer this question, the analyst provides the cost of three building standards for each geographic area: the minimum acceptable quality upgraded unit; the minimum quality new unit; and the low-cost, market-produced full unit. Each of these standards is based on a physical description of the unit.

Armed with household-group affordability and the cost of various solutions on the one hand, and the number of new and upgraded units to be produced each year on the other, the model allocates households to housing solutions following some quite simple decision rules. Then all households are classified as to whether they are assigned to solutions they can afford with their own resources or whether they have been assigned solutions that will require a subsidy. Based on these allocations and the households' corresponding investments, the main results of the model can be computed.

The fourth point that must be understood is that the model generates two key outputs in addition to the number of new and upgraded units required in each geographic area each fifth year. One is the classification of the household groups by the type of unit they can afford. Households that cannot afford the low-cost, market-produced units are designated as the "target group." The significance of the target group is that three sources of housing needs are assumed to be concentrated exclusively among target group households: overcrowding, occupancy of units to be upgraded, and occupancy of deficient units to be replaced.[3]

The remaining key output is the total investment required to meet the housing needs of the country. The model calculates this aggregate and also divides it into three parts: investment by the nontarget group, investment by target group members from their own resources, and investment that must be covered by a subsidy to the target group. Households requiring subsidies are assigned only to upgraded units or the minimum acceptable new unit (for example, a serviced site with a core unit).

It is also important to note that subsidy is defined as the value of a one-time grant necessary to close the affordability gap, as opposed to a reduction in interest rates that would last for a number of years. The cost of various housing solutions and mortgage terms are defined at full market value; hence, the gap indicates the total subsidies that would be required. Subsidies are certainly not the only way to close this gap. For example, others include inducing households to increase the share of income they spend on housing and reducing minimum building standards.

Even this brief description of the model makes it evident that investment levels will depend critically on several factors: rate of growth of households; size of initial housing deficits; income levels, income growth, share of income available for housing investments, and the capitalization terms; building standards selected; and plans for eliminating the deficits specified by the analyst. As documented in succeeding chapters, the model is ideal for analyzing the sensitivity of the outcomes to these various factors.

Notes, chapter 1

1. United Nations (1967). See Merrett (1984) for a broad conceptual discussion of such estimates.

2. A more complete description, including selected output tables and a discussion of some important underlying assumptions, is in appendix C. The available documentation is extensive and is available from the AID Document and Information Handling Facility, PPC/DCIE (SA-18, Room 209, USAID, Washington, D.C. 20523, U.S.A.).

3. The other two housing needs—newly forming households and acceptable units leaving the stock during the planning period—are assumed to be spread over all income groups.

2

HOUSING NEEDS IN 10 COUNTRIES

This chapter presents highlights from the results of the needs assessments for 10 of the countries for which the assessment tool was used. They were selected to represent a wide range of conditions within which housing needs must be met, allowing us to illustrate how outcomes can vary depending on those conditions. The number 10 was chosen to keep the exposition manageable. Because the same method was used to compute housing needs and investment for each country, any differences among countries are due, by definition, to differences in their housing, economic, or demographic conditions or to policy choices, such as their definitions of minimally acceptable housing.

A few comments on the countries provide context for the discussion. As is readily apparent from the data in table 2.1, the countries do indeed provide a wide range of locations and economic and demographic conditions. In terms of the population growth rate, for example, the three countries at one end of the spectrum (Kenya, Botswana, and Zimbabwe) have had rates of more than 3 percent per year; the three at the other end of the spectrum (Colombia, Sri Lanka, and Barbados) have had rates of less than 2 percent. A similar diversity is evident in average household incomes: in the lowest four countries it is under $2,000 per year; in the highest two countries (Panama and Ecuador) it exceeds $6,000.

17

Table 2.1 SUMMARY DATA ON POPULATION AND INCOME OF COUNTRIES STUDIED

| Country | Average annual population growth, 1970-82 (percentage) | Urban population | | Average annual growth rate as percentage of GDP, 1970-81 | Mean household income (thousand U.S. dollars)[a] |
		As percentage of total population 1982	Average annual growth rate 1970-82 (percentage)		
Barbados[b]	0.5	71	0.5	4.5	5.08
Botswana[c]	3.3	18	5.6	6.8	1.95
Colombia	1.9	65	2.7	5.4	5.54
Ecuador	2.6	46	3.8	8.1	6.45
El Salvador	3.0	41	3.4	2.2	3.83
Kenya	4.0	15	7.3	5.5	1.53
Panama	2.3	53	3.2	4.7	7.45
Peru	2.8	66	3.7	3.0	5.74
Sri Lanka	1.7	24	2.5	4.5	0.79
Zimbabwe	3.2	24	6.0	2.2	1.50

Source: World Bank (1984); reports on housing needs applications.

a. Income figures are for various years: Barbados 1980; Botswana 1984; Ecuador 1984; Kenya 1983; Panama 1982; Sri Lanka 1983; Zimbabwe 1984; Colombia 1985; El Salvador 1985; Peru 1985.
b. Growth rate for Barbados in 1985; urban population as percentage of total population in 1980.
c. Average annual growth rate for Botswana is projected growth rate for 1989; urban population as percentage of total population in 1984.

These countries also entered the 1980s with very different legacies of economic growth and urbanization. Less than a quarter of the populations of Sri Lanka and the three African countries lived in urban areas in 1982, although the cities in the African nations are growing rapidly. By contrast, the countries of Latin American already are highly urbanized. Economic growth rates are even more varied, but there is little consistency across regions.

Such diversity has important implications for housing needs. Higher population growth translates into more households and the need for more dwellings. Higher urbanization often translates into higher cost per dwelling because of the higher dwelling and infrastructure standards in urban areas. Higher household income levels and economic growth rates translates into higher levels of affordability. As explained below, these factors interact in complex ways to produce the ultimate outcomes.

A final contextual remark is in order. The results for all but 1 of the 10 countries included here are for the base case simulated in the Housing Needs Assessments, as documented in the report prepared for each country.[1] Typically, but not always, the base case embodies government policies in effect before the results of the needs assessment work were considered. But sometimes the scenario finally picked or the base case is not current policy but policy formulated in light of the information available in the simulations. Comparisons among countries, therefore, should be interpreted as illustrative of the directions of likely differences among countries rather than actual magnitudes.

The reviews of the results follow the same general format used in describing the model. Estimates of the counts of new and upgraded units required are reviewed first, followed by a look at the investment required to produce this volume of housing at building standards defined by the analyst.

NEW AND UPGRADED UNITS

Three factors drive the number of units needed in any particular year during the plan period. The first is the combination of population growth and changes in average household size, which together produce the number of new households that will be seeking shelter. The faster the population growth and the smaller the average household size, the larger the number of units needed. The second factor is the volume of housing defined as nonacceptable in the initial or base year. The larger the initial housing deficit, the more acceptable units will have to be created, through new construction or upgrading, to house everyone adequately. The third factor is the rate the analyst specifies at which deficits will be eliminated during the period. The countries involved in our field application so far almost all used the assumption that various deficits will be eliminated either at the rate of 5 percent per year, or in even increments over the 20-year period.

For classification of the initial year housing stock, table 2.2 provides information on the housing stock in each country. The distributions of units among the three categories—acceptable, upgradable, and nonupgradable—reflect the combination of the actual condition of the stock and the standards selected in doing the classification.[2]

The diversity is striking. One can contrast, for example, two countries—Ecuador and Peru—from the same region. Ecuador has a high rate of acceptable housing (almost 60 percent); about one-third of the units needs to be upgraded; about 8 percent is unsalvageable. In Peru, only 26 percent of the base year stock is rated as acceptable, nearly two-thirds is slated for upgrading, and 9 percent is deemed unsalvageable. There is no particular relationship between these distributions and average income levels in a country, reflecting, in part, the diversity in classification criteria employed.

The degree of crowding   also varies sharply—ranging from virtually none in four countries to 15 percent in Panama.[3] Within a country, crowding is always greater in urban areas, but the more urbanized countries do not exhibit consistently higher incidence of crowding than their more rural counterparts.

Table 2.2, column five expresses the total of all deficits in the initial year stock as a percent of the initial year housing stock. Countries fall into three categories: three high-income countries, with deficits ranging from 43 percent to 59 percent of the stock (Colombia, Ecuador, and Panama); four middle-income countries from various regions with deficits of about 75 percent; and three low-income countries (Sri Lanka, Zimbabwe, and Kenya) for which deficits are 87 percent to 90 percent of the initial stock. In short, while there is great country-to-country variance in the composition of the deficits, total housing deficits do appear to vary inversely with a country's income level.

Columns 7 to 9 of the same table show the distribution of construction activity in the fifth year of the plan period (the first year in the period, as noted, for which the model produces results) among three components: new construction for new households, new construction for other purposes (for example, to relieve overcrowding or replace units leaving the stock), and upgraded existing units.   There is considerable consistency in these results with the exception of Barbados and Panama. The construction of new units to house new families (33 percent to 53 percent of all construction) and upgrades (27 percent to 50 percent) are the major forms of housing investment.[4]

Countries with the highest share of new construction for new families are not invariably the ones with the highest population

Table 2.2 HOUSING STOCK AND HOUSING NEEDS, IN SELECTED COUNTRIES

Country	Quality distribution of housing stock[a]				Base Year deficit as percentage of total stock[b]	Fifth year of plan period			
	Acceptable	Non-upgradable	Upgradable	Percentage of units overcrowded		New households as percentage of total construction	Upgrades as percentage of total construction	Other construction as percentage of total construction	Total construction per 1,000 population
Bardados	29.8	2.4	67.9	4.4	74.6	22.8	64.8	12.4	13.1
Botswana	24.0	0.6	75.2	0.0	75.9	40.5	49.7	9.8	14.8
Colombia	50.9	10.4	38.6	0.0	59.0	44.2	27.2	28.6	12.8
Ecuador	58.6	5.7	35.7	2.1	43.5	43.8	29.1	27.1	12.9
El Salvador	26.6	10.5	62.9	0.0	73.4	33.9	39.9	26.2	14.2
Kenya	28.9	10.0	61.1	6.5	86.8	49.4	34.7	15.9	15.2
Panama	63.4	13.7	22.8	15.1	51.7	47.6	16.4	36.0	13.0
Peru	26.5	9.3	64.2	0.0	73.5	37.7	42.6	19.7	16.0
Sri Lanka	20.0	7.9	72.1	9.0	88.0	36.7	47.1	16.2	14.2
Zimbabwe	16.9	0.0	83.1	6.9	90.0	53.2	38.8	8.0	12.6

Note: Data presented are from "base case" analyses for each of the countries, as published in various reports.
These results are not necessarily consistent with the current housing policies of any of the countries included.
a. In base year.
b. Total deficit includes nonupgradable, upgradable, and overcrowded units.

growth rates, but there is a strong statistical correlation between the construction of new housing per thousand population and the population growth rate. As might be expected, Kenya and Zimbabwe (with their rapid population growth) are the two countries with the highest share of building activity directed to new households.

The most important influences reducing the concentration of construction activity on housing for new families are a high share of housing classified as needing to be upgraded and a low population growth rate. In Barbados and Sri Lanka both these factors are operating; in El Salvador, Peru, and Botswana high shares of housing stocks are rated upgradable, which reduces their need for new construction in spite of their medium to high population growth.

All of these points are reflected in the last column of the table, which show the total construction needed in the fifth year of the plan period per thousand population. The countries fall clearly into three groups: five with a low value, 13.1 or fewer dwellings per thousand population (Barbados, Colombia, Ecuador, Panama, Zimbabwe); three with a mid-range value (Botswana, Sri Lanka and El Salvador); and two with values exceeding 15, Kenya and Peru. It is hard to identify any simple pattern in these outcomes, but the total variance—from 12.6 to 16.0—is not as great as one might have anticipated, given the much greater differences in population growth rates and income levels.

The combination of results just presented leads to the following general conclusion. When housing needs are defined comprehensively to include replacement relief of overcrowding, upgrading, and new construction, housing needs are not simply or obviously related to simple demographic factors. Rather, the outcomes are quite sensitive to the quality distribution of the housing stock at the beginning of the period, the definitions used in classifying this stock, the rate at which units are expected to be withdrawn from the stock, and the definition of overcrowding employed.

Taken together, this means that no "rule of thumb" can be employed with confidence. Any useful assessment of the volume of new and upgraded units a country needs can be reached only after a full and careful evaluation. If a crude estimate must be made, the simple average of the total units needed per thousand population is probably the most informative, since it is the one most likely to give an estimate within 25 percent of the correct value.

HOUSING INVESTMENT

Determining the amount of investment necessary to carry out the type of housing needs outlined in the last section is inevitably somewhat complex. Several factors determine the level of investment in any year during the planning period: the average level of household incomes, the distribution of incomes, the terms on which households are able to borrow to finance housing, the minimum dwelling and infrastructure standards of the nation, and the volume of construction being undertaken. This is a large set of variables. It will simplify the discussion to look first at the relationship between the housing families in each country can afford and the cost of the minimum solutions selected by policymakers. Then the level of investment actually required to meet the estimated housing needs can be examined.

Table 2.3 summarizes the type of housing that the household in each country can afford. Recall that the analyst must specify three types of cost before estimates can be made: the average cost of improving existing units needing to be upgraded to the minimum standard, the cost of the most economical unit that is technically feasible and can meet minimum standards, and the cost of a modest

Table 2.3   DISTRIBUTION OF HOUSEHOLDS BY SOLUTIONS THEY CAN AFFORD
USING BASE CASE BUILDING STANDARDS (fifth plan year)

Country	No acceptable solution affordable	Upgrade	Minimum new unit	Full new unit	Total
	Households (%)				
Barbados	47.1[a]	23.8	23.8	5.6	100.0
Botswana	6.6	38.3	44.9	10.1	100.0
Colombia	58.2[a]	15.8	15.8	10.4	100.0
Ecuador	7.1	69.5	13.0	10.3	100.0
El Salvador	16.3	18.6	43.0	22.1	100.0
Kenya	20.2	60.6	15.9	3.2	100.0
Panama	53.5[a]	0.0	32.4	14.1	100.0
Peru	70.2[a]	5.8	20.5	3.5	100.0
Sri Lanka	7.1	71.6	19.6	1.6	100.0
Zimbabwe	0.0	13.6	80.5	5.9	100.0

Note: Data are from base case analyses for each of the countries
as published in various reports. These results are not necessarily
consistent with current housing policies of the countries.

a. The high proportion of households needing subsidy reflects
unrealistic building standards in base case analyses. See chapter
3 for further discussion.

new unit currently being offered in the market.[5]   Affordability is
determined by capitalizing the share of income that the household
can devote to housing investment—a calculation that involves
dividing households in each sector (for example, metro, urban) into
income quintiles and the mortgage terms applicable to that sector.

In table 2.3, households scheduled under the plan to have their
housing improved (so-called "incremental households") are
classified on the basis of the maximum solution they could afford
in the fifth year of the simulation period. In Barbados, for
example, only 5.6 percent of all households could afford the new
unit currently being offered in the market, whereas 23.8 percent
could afford the minimum new unit. Thus, the figures in the table

give a convenient summary of the relation between affordability and the standards selected.

The data in table 2.3 indicate that for the purposes of the needs assessment, at least four countries chose unrealistically high building standards—in the sense that the cost of upgrading an existing unit alone is out of reach for a large share of all households. In Barbados, Colombia, Panama, and Peru nearly half or more of all households are classified as being unable to afford any of the solutions. At the other end of the spectrum are three countries—Zimbabwe, Botswana, and El Salvador—for which the solutions defined are quite realistic, in that at least 40 percent of households could afford the minimum new unit.

The impact of the different standards is carried over into the housing investment figures in table 2.4. This table shows the share of all households in the target group, defined, it will be remembered, as those households that are unable to afford the low-cost market-produced unit. The figures in column 2 of the table show that the vast majority of households in all countries are in the target group. Any household with a housing need to be satisfied (for example, a newly formed household or one living in a unit "scheduled" to be upgraded) that would not be able to afford the solution assigned to it by the model is in this group by definition.

The third column shows the percentage of target group households that would not be able to afford the solution assigned to it with its own resources and, hence, would need a subsidy to realize the solution if nothing else changed. Such households are labeled as having an affordability gap.[6] The last column shows the percentage of total investment supplied by subsidies under the affordability assumptions and building standards selected by the analyst.

Table 2.4 **HOUSING INVESTMENT IN THE FIFTH YEAR FOR COUNTRIES STUDIED UNDER BASE CASE ASSUMPTIONS**

Country	Target households (thousand)	Target group as percentage of all incremental households	Percentage of target group with affordability gap[a]	Total investment as percentage of GDP	Affordability gap as percentage of total investment
Barbados	3.05	94.4	57.7	4.45	22.0
Botswana	13.66	89.1	25.6	4.47	6.0
Colombia	316.91	89.7	78.4	3.30	35.0
Ecuador	94.87	89.6	62.9	6.79	22.5
El Salvador	57.62	77.9	35.1	5.63	2.6
Kenya	277.51	96.8	61.7	11.94	31.9
Panama	22.43	85.9	62.3	5.42	14.4
Peru	277.21	96.5	77.0	3.93	36.2
Sri Lanka	215.77	98.4	45.7	4.36	17.8
Zimbabwe	94.3	94.1	14.3	5.87	2.1

Note: Data are from base case analyses for each of the countries, as published in various reports. These results are not necessarily consistent with current housing policies of the countries.

a. The affordability gap is the difference between the cost of the housing solution (upgrade or minimum new unit) to which the household has been assigned and the housing investment the household can afford with its own resources.

Different patterns emerge for the groups of countries with sharply divergent building standards relative to affordable costs. For the four countries with quite high standards, 69 percent of households in the target group have affordability gaps and need subsidies, and the subsidies would account for 24 percent of total investment. In contrast, for the three countries with highly realistic standards, 25 percent of all target group households need subsidies, and only 3.5 percent of all investment is attributed to subsidies. Thus the building standards selected powerfully effect the size of the role that government is likely to have to play to meet the country's housing needs.

The ratio of housing investment (HI) to GDP is a useful measure of a country's investment activity in the housing sector. It has the virtues of controlling for the overall level of income (although not its distribution among various parts of the population) and avoiding exchange rate issues in making cross-country comparisons. The HI to GDP ratio is given in the fourth column of table 2.4. In general, between 3.3 percent and 5.8 percent of GDP would have to go to the housing sector. The two exceptions are Kenya and Ecuador, because of the high percentage of GDP needed for housing under their base case plans. This is well within the range typical for middle- to high-income countries and one potentially within the range of all these countries.

No straightforward relationship appears between either HI/GDP and building standards or between HI/GDP and per capita GNP or average household income, even though the latter relationship was documented by Burns and Grebler in their classic study (1977, ch. 2).

Rather, the strong relationship is between population growth rates and HI/GDP. For the four countries in this group with population growth rates of at least 3.0 percent in recent years, the ratio is 6.9 percent, while the similar figure for the three countries with population growth rates of less than 2 percent is 4.0 percent.[7]

Hence, population growth does appear to have the clearest simple effect on the level of investment necessary for developing nations to meet their housing needs. Population growth has a smaller effect on the number of acceptable units required, however. The reason for this difference seems to lie in the substantially higher cost per unit of new housing—which is associated with population growth—than with the cost of upgrading existing housing. In effect, new units are being weighed more heavily in the investment than in the total unit calculations, which permits the kind of correlation observed between investment and population growth rates.[8]

Notes, chapter 2

1. The exception is Zimbabwe, which used an alternative estimate that permitted households to contain lodgers and not be considered overcrowded.

2. A summary of the definitions used in classifying the stock in each country is presented in appendix A.

3. It should be noted that in some cases the rating of "no overcrowding" simply reflects lack of information.

4. Panama is a special case because of its exceptional share of unsalvageable and overcrowded units; Barbados is also because of the extraordinary share of construction activity accounted for by upgrades.

5. These three cost levels are specified separately for metro, other urban, and rural areas. The standards adopted by each country are outlined in appendix A.

6. Not all households are assigned a unit they can afford. An example may clarify the point. Many more households may be able to

afford at most an upgraded unit than there are such units scheduled to be upgraded.   The "excess" households are allocated to new units, which they cannot afford.   See appendix C for details.

7. The simple correlation for the full sample of 14 countries between HI/GDP and the population growth rate (1970-82) is 0.56.
   Note that these high-growth countries include two--Botswana and Zimbabwe--that were cited as having realistic building standards; the correlation is not spurious, however, because high population growth acts as a proxy for high standards.

8. We also expect that an analysis which involved many more countries than were available for this analysis would document the importance of other factors such as the level of economic development and the building standards selected.

3

WHAT DRIVES HOUSING NEEDS?

Some salient points have emerged from this quick review of housing needs for 10 countries, but a sense of frustration may persist from being unable to identify more clearly the most powerful factors affecting housing needs. This chapter examines and compares five factors that have been advanced by various analysts as having potentially strong impacts on housing needs. For expositional purposes, these factors have been combined into two groups:

● Differences in population growth rates and the rate of growth of urban areas. As discussed below, both factors affect the number of new and upgraded units needed and the corresponding level of investment.

● Differences that affect only the level of investment; the candidates here are the share of household income devoted to housing investment, mortgage interest rates, and the minimum building standards selected by a country.

The general technique employed has been to simulate, for a group of countries, a solution in which a policy or other factor has been changed and to compute the impact of the change by comparing the "base case" and "policy" results. Not all alternatives have been simulated for all countries, both to keep the volume of simulations manageable and to allow concentration on more interesting cases. These five cases will be reviewed in order, including comparisons among the impacts of the various factors. The final section makes some policy-oriented observations about the findings.

CHANGES IN POPULATION AND URBANIZATION

Changes in the rate of population growth have a significant impact. In particular, the average population growth rate for the first five years of the planning period of the four "medium growth rate" countries was applied in the sample of 10 countries to all of the countries. Questions then could be addressed such as: how would Sri Lanka's housing needs change if it had the population growth rate of Ecuador and similar countries? Specifically, the separate average growth rates for urban and rural areas for these four countries were used in each country.

The original and revised countrywide population growth rates are shown in the first two columns of table 3.1. The revised growth rates differ among the countries, depending on their degree or urbanization, since different urban and rural growth rates are being used. As evident from the figures, there are major changes in the growth rates for Barbados and Sri Lanka among the slow-growing countries and also among all of the high growth rate countries.

The change in the future population growth rate was the only change that has been made. An important implication of changing only this rate is that household incomes will also change, since the same national income is being divided among fewer or more households.[1] The income shifts are not dramatic, however, since only the future growth rate is being changed.

The balance of table 3.1 presents figures summarizing the impact of these changes. Before discussing the results themselves, a couple of words on the type of data presented are in order, since the same format is used for all of the results. First, the results are for the fifth year in the 20-year planning period. Second, percentage changes from the base case are presented for several key outputs, for example, total housing needs (in number of units).

Table 3.1   IMPACT OF STANDARD POPULATION GROWTH RATE ON HOUSING NEEDS

	Base case average actual population growth rate in fifth year	Average standard population growth rate in fifth year	Percentage difference from base case				Elasticities with respect to population growth rate			
			Housing needs	Households needing subsidy	Total housing investment	Subsidy requirement	Housing needs	Households needing subsidy	Total housing investment	Subsidy requirement
Low growth rate										
Barbados	0.52	2.52	44.6	49.1	59.4	93.2	.11	.13	.15	.24
Colombia	1.83	2.46	10.9	12.4	11.5	18.6	.33	.38	.35	.56
Sri Lanka	1.60	2.93	21.4	38.7	24.5	58.0	.26	.47	.30	.70
Medium growth rate										
Ecuador	2.32	2.39	-1.2	2.0	0.6	2.7	.40	.67	.20	.90
El Salvador	2.47	2.20	-3.2	-2.4	-4.6	-1.2	.29	.22	.42	.11
Panama	2.11	2.24	2.5	1.6	3.1	2.4	.42	.27	.52	.40
Peru	2.54	2.48	-0.5	-0.3	-3.2	-4.4	.25	.15	1.60	2.20
High growth rate										
Botswana	3.30	1.87	-19.6	33.9	-23.0	-42.8	.45	.79	.53	1.00
Kenya	3.86	1.57	-31.1	-36.6	-41.8	-49.4	.52	.62	.71	.84
Zimbabwe	3.51	1.79	-26.8	-78.7	-31.0	-81.8	.54	1.60	.63	1.67

Note: The standard population growth rate was derived from the weighted average of growth rates in urban and metropolitan areas and rural areas of medium-growth rate countries in the study, i.e., Ecuador, El Salvador, Panama, and Peru.

Third, "elasticities" were used for the same output measures. An elasticity is a ratio of percentage changes. Perhaps an illustration best explains this concept. The elasticity of total housing needs with respect to the population growth rate is the percentage change in total housing needs that would be associated with a 1 percent change in the population growth rate.

Elasticities produce numbers that indicate the amount of change in the output independent of the size of the change in the causal factor, in this case the population growth rate. The table shows that for Barbados the elasticity of housing needs with respect to the population growth rate has a value of 0.11, that is, a 1 percent change in the population growth rate is associated with a 0.11 percent change in total housing needs. The comparable figure for Sri Lanka is 0.26. To see the value of using this measure, contrast the two elasticities with the simple percentage change in total needs associated with the change in population growth rates for these two countries (column 3). The values are 44.6 percent for Barbados and 21.4 percent for Sri Lanka. The results differ widely from the elasticities because they have not been standardized for the extent of change in the population growth rates in the two countries.

Because the elasticities control for the degree of change in the "causal variable"—in this case the population growth rate—we emphasize this measure in the discussion of the results. In general, the greater the value of the elasticity, the greater the impact a percentage change in the "causal factor" on the variable under consideration. Also, the elasticities are expressed in absolute terms: the direction of change was ignored because the primary interest is in the magnitude of the impacts involved.

The effects of standardizing urban and rural population growth rates, as measured by the elasticities, reveal that total housing needs do not respond very strongly to a change in population growth. That is, a 10 percent change in the population growth rate, say from 2.0 percent to 2.2 percent per year, is associated with only a 1 percent to 5 percent change in total needs. This result is understandable, given the other factors at work, especially the sources of housing needs other than newly forming households. There are comparable impacts from a change in population growth on the number of households receiving subsidies.

Population growth changes have somewhat greater impacts on total investment and on the volume of subsidies required to meet fully the housing needs defined. The range of response is greater and the average value of the elasticity is higher: the mean of the elasticities of total housing needs with respect to population growth is 0.36, while the comparable figures for total housing investment and subsidies are 0.54 and 0.85, respectively. The difference is due to the extra effect that changing household incomes brings to bear.

A final key point about changes in the population growth rates distinguishes them from many other changes: their impact continues to grow year after year. In contrast, a shift in mortgage interest rates or the share of income spent on housing, as examples, cause a one-time change: a shift in the level of housing families can afford. The figures just reviewed were of the impact after a change in the population growth rate had been sustained for five years. Below are listed several average elasticities for the 10 countries studied for sustaining the same changes for 10 years as well as the 5-year figures presented earlier.

	Average elasticities	
Changes in	5 years	10 years
Housing needs	.36	.80
Investment	.54	.77
Subsidies needed	.85	1.28

As is readily apparent, the size of impact increases steadily with the passage of time.   Hence, the benefits of lower population growth in reducing the housing problems a nation must confront cumulate in a way which they do not for most other types of change.

Changes in the rate of urbanization lead to much smaller impacts on housing needs and associated investment than does population change.   In principle, a higher rate of population growth in cities (called a "higher rate of urbanization" in this section) can have two effects. First, since urban household sizes often differ from rural ones, a shift of population changes the number of households seeking shelter nationwide.   Second, because infrastructure standards often must be higher in cities to accommodate safely higher density populations, the   costs of minimum acceptable solutions are higher; this raises the investment required to meet housing needs.

With these two factors in mind, we selected four countries that represent a good range of values for the ratio of urban to rural costs of minimum solutions and for household sizes. The values of these ratios for the four countries shown are in the third and fourth columns of table 3.2.

The change in urbanization was determined by diverting one-half the growth in the rural population that occurred in the base case during the first five years of the simulation period to urban areas.[2] Hence, the increase in urban population depended on rural population growth rates and the share of the population in rural areas. For this reason, Kenya experiences a jump in the share of the population living in urban areas while the other three countries included exhibit much smaller changes (see the first two columns of the table).

A quick study of the elasticities in the last set of columns in the table documents the comparatively anemic effects produced by

Table 3.2 IMPACT OF INCREASED URBANIZATION

| Country | Percentage of population in urban areas | | Ratio of construction costs[a] | Ratio of household size[b] | Percentage difference from base | | | | Elasticity with respect to urbanization change[c] | | | |
	Base	Policy			Total housing needs	Households needing subsidy	Total housing investment	Total subsidy	Total housing needs	Households needing subsidy	Total housing investment	Total subsidy
El Salvador	53.7	58.4	3.12	.77	2.3	-2.4	7.4	13.2	.07	.07	.23	.41
Kenya	19.1	31.8	2.30	.75	7.1	20.8	38.5	103.2	.05	.14	.26	.71
Panama	57.0	60.0	1.14	.90	.7	.6	1.5	1.7	.04	.03	.08	.09
Peru	72.3	73.3	4.55	1.19	-0.1	-.2	1.4	2.3	d	d	.07	.12

Note: Urbanization increased by shifting half of the incremental rural population to metropolitan and other urban areas over the first 10 years of the planning period.
a. Ratio of the design cost of the minimum new unit in the urban areas to cost in rural areas.
b. Ratio of average household size in urban areas to size in rural areas.
c. Urbanization defined as the percent of population living in urban areas.
d. Less than .005.

increased urbanization.   The   average   elasticity of urbanization with respect to   total   housing   needs   is   only   0.04.   Comparable elasticities for total housing   investment   and total subsidies are 0.16 and 0.33, respectively.   These   are   small values in both an absolute sense and in   comparison   with those for population growth rates.[3]

HOUSING AFFORDABILITY

Three main factors influence   the affordability of housing: changes in   the   share   of   income   that   households   devote   to   housing expenditures, changes in   mortgage   interest   rates, and changes in the cost of different housing solutions.[4]

It is convenient   to   discuss   the   first   two   of these factors together, since the same countries and   the same type of change are employed in both   cases.   The   half-dozen countries included were selected to give a   good   range   of income levels and affordability patterns.   For both   the   share   of   income   devoted to housing and mortgage interest rates, a 15   percent change was invoked from base case values.   For share   of   income,   the   share of income going to housing was increased   by   15   percent   only   for households in the lowest three income quintiles.   Restricting the increase to these lower income   groups   is   consistent   with   the   idea   that if such households had an opportunity to   occupy good quality housing, many would be   willing   to   spend   more   of   their   income   on   it.[5]   In contrast, the applicable mortgage interest rate has been reduced by 15 percent for households   in   all   income   groups.   This reduction should be attributed to a   reduction in inflation, for example, and not to   a   general   subsidy.   Both   changes   have   the   effect of increasing the value of housing that households can afford.

The results of these simulations are summarized in tables 3.3 and 3.4. No results are reported for total housing needs, since total needs are not affected by changes of the type being considered here. In the results for both changes, the average elasticities for total investment are considerably smaller than those for total subsidies; the average values for the total investment elasticities in the two cases are about 0.3 and 0.5, while those for total subsidies are about 1.5. This pattern makes sense since, when the affordability of those receiving subsidies in the base case increases, the principal effect is to substitute private investment for government subsidies, leaving total investment largely unaffected.[6] The major source of change for total investment comes from the expenditures of households receiving subsidies in the base case.[7]

The impact of the changes in interest rates and the share of income going to housing can also be compared with that of changing the population growth rate. The impact of all three changes on total housing investment is about the same. However, changes in the population growth rate have only about half of the effect on total subsidies required as do shifts in the share of income going to housing or the effective mortgage interest rate.

The final case is that of reducing the cost of the minimum upgraded unit and the minimum new unit. Five countries were included in these simulations, on the basis of their having comparatively high costs for these solutions in the base case.[8] In two countries, Kenya and Zimbabwe, only the costs of the solutions in urban areas appeared high; only these costs were reduced. In every instance in which costs were cut, the reduction was a uniform 25 percent.

The results of lowering the standards embodied in the minimum solutions (shown in table 3.5) are quite similar to those just

Table 3.3 IMPACT OF AN INCREASE IN SHARE OF INCOME DEVOTED TO HOUSING BY LOWER INCOME HOUSEHOLDS

Country	Percentage change from base case			Elasticity with respect to share of income to housing		
	Households needing subsidy	Total housing investment	Total subsidy	Households needing subsidy	Total housing investment	Total subsidy
Botswana	0.0	3.0	-13.4	0.0	0.20	0.89
Colombia	0.0	0.4	-9.4	0.0	0.27	0.63
Ecuador	0.0	0.9	-13.2	0.0	0.60	0.88
Peru	-5.6	0.5	-6.0	0.37	0.03	0.40
Sri Lanka	-21.7	0.4	-28.5	1.45	0.03	1.90
Zimbabwe	-50.0	2.9	-71.4	3.33	0.19	4.76

Note: Share of income going to housing increased by 15 percent over the base for the lower three income quintiles.

Table 3.4   IMPACT OF INCREASING CREDIT AVAILABILITY TO REDUCE MORTGAGE
            INTEREST RATE

| | Percentage difference from base case | | | Elasticity with respect to interest rate change | | |
Country	Households needing subsidy	Total housing investment	Total subsidy	Households needing subsidy	Total housing investment	Total subsidy
Botswana	0.0	10.6	-10.4	0.0	0.71	0.69
Colombia	0.0	7.7	-10.8	0.0	0.51	0.72
Ecuador	-8.2	2.6	-13.8	0.55	0.17	0.92
Peru	-16.0	7.0	-11.3	1.07	0.47	0.75
Sri Lanka	-18.4	4.5	-22.6	1.23	0.30	1.51
Zimbabwe	-35.1	12.2	-67.4	2.34	0.81	4.49

Note: Reduction is 15 percent of base case interest rate in each sector.

Table 3.5   IMPACT OF LOWER COST HOUSING SOLUTIONS

Country	Percentage difference from base case			Cost change elasticity		
	Households needing subsidy	Total housing investment	Total subsidy	Households needing subsidy	Total housing investment	Total subsidy
Barbados	-9.1	-9.0	-40.9	0.36	0.36	1.64
Colombia	0.0	-13.4	-38.2	0.00	0.54	1.53
Kenya[a]	-23.9	-15.1	-41.0	0.96	0.60	1.64
Panama	-36.8	-5.6	-38.6	1.47	0.22	1.54
Zimbabwe[a]	-100.0	-2.0	-100.0	4.00	0.08	4.00

a. Reduction applied to urban areas only. Results reported are for urban areas only.

reviewed for increasing housing affordability.   The average of the
elasticities of total   housing   investment   with respect to changed
solution costs is about 0.3;   that for total subsidies with respect
to changed solution costs, about   1.7.   The impact of changing the
solution costs on subsidies is   the   largest of any factor that has
been considered.[9]   The   powerful   impact   of   reduced standards is
especially   worth   of   attention   because   it   is   fully controlled
government tool that can be applied quickly.   These aspects make it
almost unique.

POLICY IMPLICATIONS

Based on the summary   figures   in   table   3.6   and on the foregoing
discussion, several concluding observations seem warranted.[10]

● It is more difficult to reduce total housing needs than the level
of housing investment or housing subsidies.   The greater difficulty
for   housing   needs   arises   from   the   comparative   paucity   of
instruments available to affect   housing needs and the instruments'
comparatively modest short-term quantitative effects.

● Reducing population growth is a key long-term element in reducing
housing investment requirements   and   the   subsidies   that would be
necessary if government   committed   itself   to   meeting   all of its
country's housing   needs.   This   analysis   suggests   that reduced
population growth rates   will   be   more   effective   in limiting the
total   amount   of   investment   necessary   to   meet   housing needs,
compared to other policies that   might be pursued, than in reducing
subsidy requirements.   Population   reductions   will have more potent
impacts the longer they are sustained.

● Reduction in the required   subsidies   (or closing the gap between
what lower income households   can   afford   and   the cost of minimum
housing solutions) is highly   responsive   to   three changes: lower
design standards, increased credit   availability   to reduce mortgage
interest rates, and increased share of income devoted to housing by
those who would receive the subsidies.

Lowering the minimum   acceptable   housing   standards is the tool
most immediately at   government's   disposal.   Many countries have

Table 3.6 SUMMARY OF THE IMPACTS OF CHANGES IN SELECTED FACTORS ON
HOUSING NEEDS, INVESTMENT, AND SUBSIDIES
(average elasticities)

Causal factor	Total needs	Total investment	Total subsidies
Population growth rate	0.38	0.54	0.85
Rate of urbanization	0.04	0.16	0.33
Share of income spent on housing[a]	--	0.32	1.57
Credit availability and mortgage interest rate	--	0.50	1.51
Cost of minimally acceptable housing solutions	--	0.30	1.72

a. Change affecting households in the lowest three income
quintiles only.
-- Not applicable.

adopted such standards, but many others have considerable room for
reductions, at least for a "starter solution."

Increasing credit availability to reduce mortgage interest rates
offers another alternative.   This does not mean cutting rates
through subsidies that would just replace one subsidy with another.
The main target of opportunity is probably in making market-rate,
formal housing loans available to lower income households which do
not now have access to such funds.   While a good deal is made of
informal financial markets serving the poor, precious little is
known about how the poor finance their housing.   What is known
suggests that coverage is spotty at best, and costs can be high
compared to formal sector rates.[11]   In most developing countries,
increasing the supply of mortgage credit will require major changes
in the housing finance system, and possibly financial markets
generally, for the housing sector to compete openly for funds.   On
balance, reductions in mortgage interest rates offer a good deal of

promise in closing the affordability gap. Realizing this potential will, however, demand years of sustained effort.

Increasing the share of income devoted to housing by people needing subsidies may be quite difficult. Naturally, the key is to offer sufficiently attractive housing that families will make necessary sacrifices to live there.   For many poor families who have lived in utter squalor, this willingness may well be present. In the past, however, some sites and service projects employed excessively high standards (and assumed too great a willingness on the part of participants to allocate income to housing). This resulted in a combination of unintended subsidies and the eventual exclusion of target beneficiaries from the project (Mayo 1985). This experience suggests that government must use great caution in attempting to induce households to increase the share of income spent on housing to close the affordability gap.

Notes, chapter 3

1. It is arguable that increased or decreased population would have some corresponding impact on aggregate GDP.   This may be the case, but, for simplicity, this point was ignored.

2. The increased urban population was divided evenly between metro and other urban areas.

3. Sustained changes in urbanization will have cumulative effects similar to those presented above for population growth rate changes.

4. Mortgage interest rates are the same rates used in the case of incremental housing building or improvements to compute the present value of the streams of investment (see appendix C).

5. For more on affordability and housing demand in developing countries, see Malpezzi and Mayo (1985), and Keare and Parris (1983).

6. This is the appropriate place to comment on the fact that, for many policy simulations, the effect on the number of households needing subsidies seems either quite small or too large. This results from the use of income quintiles. To amplify somewhat on this point, if the model divided households into more income groups for these calculations, say 10 or even 20 groups, some reduction in the number of households needing subsidies would be recorded in all countries. It is only the income averaging within each income quintile that keeps households in the base case--with incomes just below the level needing a subsidy--from moving out of this category when their housing affordability increases.

Similarly, there are cases in which the amount of change from a change in affordability is, in effect, overstated. This happens when the households in an income quintile have an affordability level in the base case very close to the cost of a higher quality housing solution. A small change in affordability then places all of these households in the higher category, thus overstating the impact of the policy change. This type of "lumpiness" or integer problem is endemic to models that divide households and solutions into a small number of categories. The decision to use income quintiles in the housing needs model was based largely on our views about the reliability of income distribution data. For both types of change, the number of households needing subsidies declines in some countries and in others remains unchanged. This difference in results is something of an artifact, caused by the use of a small number of income groups in the affordability calculations.

7. The elasticity of total investment with respect to interest-rate change is greater than the similar elasticity with respect to share of income devoted to housing because the interest rate changes apply to all households whereas the changes in housing expenditures apply only to those in the lowest three income quintiles.

8. The procedure for deciding which countries to include in this analysis was somewhat arbitrary. After looking at the cost of solutions for all countries, two rules appeared to make sense for identifying those with comparatively high costs. First, costs were deemed to be potentially high if the cost of an upgrade exceeded at least $600 and a new unit $1,800. Second, the ratio of the cost of the solution to average annual household income exceeded 0.3 for upgrades and 0.5 for new units. These rules were always applied together. Hence, a country would not have been included if upgrading a unit cost less than $600, although it meant that the cost to income ratio was 0.4. More data on affordability are presented in appendix A.

9. Although not reported here, we also analyzed the effects of raising real GDP growth rates. We simulated an incremental 0.5 percent per year increase in real GDP growth for six countries (El Salvador, Zimbabwe, Colombia, Sri Lanka, Botswana, Ecuador, and Peru). Sustaining this incremental growth for five years produced average elasticity values similar to those for the other factors analyzed which directly affect affordability. Changes in income growth rates, like changes in population growth rates, have a self-reinforcing effect. Hence, higher economic growth sustained over a decade would produce proportionately greater changes than those produced by the other affordability factors, all of which have "one-time" effects.

10. Admittedly these are rough-and-ready comparisons, since the averages of the elasticities reported are generally for different sets of countries. We have done more refined comparisons, however, for comparable sets of countries where possible; and the same general patterns emerge.

11. For further discussion of this point, see Struyk and Turner (1986).

4

APPLYING THE NEEDS MODEL: POLICY OUTCOMES AND LESSONS

The foregoing chapters demonstrate that much can be learned from
analyzing the determinants of housing needs across a set of
countries. Now our focus shifts to the experience of individual
countries in applying the model.   We address two especially
important questions:

● What impact did applying the housing needs assessment method have
in these countries, especially on their housing policies?

● What lessons do these applications yield for other countries that
might like to use the model to help them reconsider their housing
policies?

Clearly, the first question tops the list for host country
policymakers and the donor community.   The second question becomes
urgent if the payoff from the past applications encourages other
countries to undertake similar applications.

To acquire the information needed to address these questions we
developed a questionnaire about individual experiences applying the
needs model.   This questionnaire was sent to 78 persons in 15
countries where the model had been applied.[1]   The selection of
respondents was made by asking the consultants who led the
applications in each host country for names of the persons involved
and checking these lists with staff members at the Regional Offices
of the Office of Housing and Urban Programs, U.S. Agency for
International Development (USAID), who had participated in many of

the applications.   Since the application to Jamaica was never completed, most of the discussion is restricted to the other 14 countries.

We received a total of 37 responses, after various forms of followup. The response rate was higher for consultants who worked on the applications and for USAID staff than for individuals in the host counties. An important factor associated with the response rate in individual countries seems to have been the degree of exposure of the completed needs estimates in policy discussions. (The number of responses received are tabulated by country at the end of appendix D.) We have not been able to verify the accuracy of these responses but believe that the information given is reliable.

IMPACT ON POLICY DEBATE AND CHANGE

The success of any study on changing a country's policies is inevitably difficult to "score," since so many circumstances can influence the outcomes. Timing of the presentation of results can, for instance, be critical, as can access to senior officials by persons working on the study.   These conditions differed widely among the 15 countries, yielding a realistic cross-section of what might be expected in future applications.

The various outcomes are summarized in table 4.1 on a country-by-country basis under two headings--"overall benefits" and "policy changes." In general, a review of the entries in this table suggest that in three countries--Barbados, Educador, and Zimbabwe--applying the model had a major impact.   In four countries (El Salvador, Panama, Peru, and Turkey), the application of the model seems to have had little benefit.   The remaining seven countries fall somewhere in between.

The discussion begins with the broader category of benefits, which explicitly recognizes that important gains—other than direct effects on policy—can materialize from this type of exercise. The entries in table 4.1 show two commonly cited areas: establishing the scale of a country's housing problems and providing a comprehensive look at its overall housing situation. In many countries, the size-of-problem estimates have appeared in government documents describing the housing sector and government policy. And in several, the total housing investment and subsidy requirements necessary to meet the country's housing needs were considered valuable, and the results generally led to discussions within government on whether the minimum housing standards chosen were indeed reasonable and achievable under expected resource constraints.

The value of the perspective provided by the housing assessment tool was presumably greatest in countries where the needs estimates served as the foundation for developing a national housing strategy: Barbados, Kenya, and Jordan. In terms of associating policy change with the results of the housing needs assessment the three countries shared a common pattern. In all three, the changes focused on lowering what government had defined as minimum acceptable standards to reduce the housing sector's total investment requirements and cut the volume of subsidies implied. There were some additional changes as well which differed according to the country. In Barbados, for instance, government activity shifted from direct housing development to a financing role. In Ecuador the government changed its decision to pursue a housing strategy with high per unit subsidies. In Zimbabwe officials were induced to rethink the housing standards they had specified as "normal."

Table 4.1 PERCEIVED OVERALL BENEFITS AND POLICY CHANGES ASSOCIATED WITH APPLYING THE HOUSING NEEDS MODEL

Country	Overall benefits	Policy changes
Barbados	• Established orders-of-magnitude of sector costs. • Forced government to make decisions about data inputs and some policies. • Forced Ministry to consider finance aspects of housing more fully.	• Set more realistic building standards. • Shifted government resources from capital projects to financing housing for lower income households privately developed.
Botswana	• Offered first comprehensive look at the country's housing situation. • Caused serious discussion about expanding role of the private sector.	• No specific changes attributable.
Colombia	• Provoked discussions about the roles of different institutions in addressing target groups.	• No specific changes attributable.
Costa Rica	• Caused discussion within government about level of subsidies required to achieve housing goals and on minimum unit size.	• Too soon to tell; application done in 1986.
El Salvador	• No specific benefits attributable	• No specific changes attributable.
Ecuador	• Served as basis for policy discussions with new administration; standards were explicit issue. • Instrumental in appraisal of new donor project.	• Helped convince government to reduce subsidies and emphasize progressive housing construction (vs. initial construction of full units).
Honduras	• Defined housing problem as larger than anticipated. • Caused discussions within government with regard to standards, location (urban/rural) of government assistance, and subsidy levels.	• Follow-up work underway; too soon to tell.
Jordan	• Established overall framework for policy discussion and identifying areas for further investigation. • Use began as organizing device in developing national housing strategy.	• Too soon to tell; strategy development still underway.

Table 4.1 (continued)

Country	Overall benefits	Policy changes
Kenya	• Caused serious discussion within government of cost of minimum housing solutions and building and infrastructure standards required by local authorities. • Provided framework for national housing strategy.	• Too soon to tell; strategy development still underway.
Panama	• Helped set stage for policy discussions. • Cited in government documents.	• No specific changes attributable.
Peru	• Caused some discussions within government on conflict between resources available and housing needs.	• No specific changes attributable.
Sri Lanka	• Allowed policymakers to assess dimensions of true housing needs quantitatively. • Provided realistic estimate of costs of comprehensive improvement program.	• No specific changes attributable.
Turkey	• No specific benefits attributable	• No specific changes attributable.
Zimbabwe	• Stimulated debate about housing policy, especially building standards for rural areas. • Used in cabinet paper on housing policy (1986) and other government documents. • Provided comprehensive framework.	• Had perceptible impact on future housing policy in the area of building standards.

This probably is the lower limit of the ultimate effectiveness of the needs assessments on housing policy because the model was applied in several countries as early as 1986, providing insufficient time for any important policy changes to materialize. In many countries, indeed, major policy changes require years of consensus building before they actually occur—a process which may be going in some of the countries included in this analysis. The estimates can also serve as a continuing resource to be used in the policy process.   The housing needs estimates for Kenya done in 1984, for example, were used in 1986–87 in the formulation of a new national housing strategy.

What about the four countries where the assessment seems to have had little or no impact?   The housing assessments were independent exercises in all three of the countries where policies were substantially affected.   In all four of the applications with little apparent effect the housing needs assessment was part of a larger study, generally a sector study (see table 4.2). When buried in documents with larger coverage, the needs estimates often receive little attention.   El Salvador's current situation made examination of long-term programs especially difficult.

In two of every three countries where the model has been applied, the results have stirred some debate and been helpful in governmental planning exercises.   In one out of five, the model had an immediate influence on the country's housing policies; long-term policy effects may yet materialize in other countries. The next section looks more closely at selected aspects of the application process with an eye to increasing effectiveness.

Table 4.2   CONTEXT OF HOUSING NEEDS ASSESSMENT IN COUNTRIES WITH
LITTLE APPARENT EFFECT

Country	If part of larger project, type of project	Other notable circumstances
El Salvador	Shelter sector assessment	Armed conflict has reduced current data available
Panama	Urban development assessment[a]	
Peru	Shelter sector assessment[b]	
Turkey	More general sectoral analysis	

a. This is an overview of the system of urban areas in a country,
including finances, administration, and provision of infrastructure
services.
b. This is a general overview of the housing sector, including
public and private institutions active in the sector.

SUCCESSFUL APPLICATION OF THE MODEL

One key to successful application may be for all parties involved
to understand the primary purpose of the application and the
principal audience.   Three different, but related purposes for
applying the model can be defined:

● generating or constructively entering a policy debate

● doing a solid technical assessment for use by others for planning
and policy considerations

● training host country individuals in using the model.

Multiple audiences can also be readily identified.   The main
audiences include: headquarter donor staff, donor staff assigned
to the host country, and local officials and host country
officials.

The questionnaire asked respondents to rank their perception of the primary objective and audience for the needs assessment (see table 4.3). They were asked to do this ranking twice, once based on their perception before applying the model and once given their perceptions after application. A good deal of shifting occurred in the "before" and "after" rankings.

The lack of apparent consistency about expressed priorities was conspicuous. In 3 countries there was serious disagreement among the respondents about the ratings of primary objectives. Among the remaining 11 countries, respondents from 8 ranked entering the results into the policy dialogue as the first priority. Even less agreement was evident as to the primary audience. The respondents in 5 disagreed among themselves. Among the balance, there was an almost even split among the three options—headquarter donor officials, local officials, and local donor staff in the host country.

The fact that there was no strong pattern of agreement about the primary objective or audience even among the three countries where fairly immediate policy changes were associated with the application of the model led us to look a little further into probable reasons why. The additional information made the lack of apparent consensus less puzzling.

In Barbados, the principal objective was reported as a good technical assessment. In fact, the estimates were fed into a process for developing a new national housing strategy: the policy linkage was already assured. In Ecuador, and to a lesser degree in Zimbabwe, influencing policy was emphasized. This suggests the rankings gleaned from the interviews should be treated with some caution. However, at the very least, the lack of agreement—especially about the identity of the primary audience—indicates that a better job could be done in defining goals before beginning to apply the model.

Table 4.3   **RANKING OF OBJECTIVES AND AUDIENCE**

	Primary objective			Primary audience		
	Strong technical assessment	Policy dialogue	Training	Host country officials	USAID Washington	Other USAID
Barbados	1	2	3	No agreement among respondents		2
Botswana	2	1	3	1	3	2
Colombia	—	1	—	1	2	
Costa Rica	2	1	2	No agreement among respondents		
El Salvador	2	1	3	2	3	1
Ecuador	2	1	3	No agreement among respondents		2
Honduras	3	1	3	2	1	2
Jordan	3	1	2	1	3	
Kenya	No agreement among respondents		2	No agreement among respondents		
Panama	1	3	2	No agreement among respondents		
Peru	2	1	3	2	1	
Sri Lanka	No agreement among respondents		1	3	1	1
Turkey	Disagreement between these two			3	1	2
Zimbabwe	3	3		1	2	2

Note: 1 = highest priority;   3 = lowest priority.

It should also be noted that data problems are a potentially serious impediment to a technically sound application. Despite reports by respondents of excellent cooperation from government agencies and other data sources, significant data problems were encountered in the majority of countries (see table 4.4). Only four countries reported no serious difficulties. The most common problem was in assembling data on income distribution by geographic sector; up-to-date information and appropriate data were both lacking. For example, only data on salaried employees or income tax payers would be available, or only national or urban figures could be found. Information was also scanty on the division of the existing housing stock among quality categories and total investment in the housing sector.

None of the problems was so severe, except in Jamaica, that the assessment could not be completed with the aid of sensitivity analysis with alternative values for the suspect inputs. In their responses, several consultants emphasized the importance of checking all possible sources of data at donor agencies before going to the field as one way of mitigating data problems.

In 7 of the 15 applications included in this section, formal advisory panels proved useful as forums in which to obtain guidance on data issues and to present initial results. The people involved with these panels were enthusiastic about their usefulness and some even rated them as the sine qua non of a successful application. Our experience does not yield such a strong conclusion, however, since several successful analyses were done without advisory panels, including two out of the three most successful applications (Barbados and Ecuador).

In nearly all cases, the way the model was applied was for one or more consultants to visit a country for several weeks. During this period they took the lead in gathering data, entering the data in the model, doing the initial simulations, and discussing the

Table 4.4   DATA INPUTS THAT WERE DIFFICULT TO ASSEMBLE

Barbados	Income distribution housing expenditures, housing quality distribution, housing decay rates
Botswana	Housing quality distribution
Colombia	None
Costa Rica	Share of housing expenditures that are recurring expenses
El Salvador	All data difficult except costs of housing solutions and financing terms
Ecuador	None
Honduras	Income distribution, quality distribution of the housing stock, shelter costs, sector housing investment
Jamaica	Income distribution, quality distribution of the housing stock, share of income spent on housing, total housing investment
Jordan	Share of income spent on housing, decay rate for upgradable housing
Kenya	Income distribution, income growth, housing investment
Panama	Income distribution
Peru	None
Sri Lanka	None
Turkey	Income distribution, housing quality distribution
Zimbabwe	Income distribution, housing quality distribution

initial results. Local USAID staff and host–country officials were involved to varying degrees in each of these steps. Copies of the reports, which consultants completed after returning home, were sent to the countries studied, typically to the local USAID office.

Several respondents suggested that the needs assessment would be more widely used if this process were modified. In particular, they suggested adding a second field visit after transmittal of the draft report. The purpose of such a visit would be to present the results in a seminar, do training on the model, and run additional policy simulations of direct interest to local officials. Before the second visit, country personnel could digest the report and think about changes they might want to make in the simulations, which many in the field see as important to attracting and sustaining interest.

In practice, this two–phase process occurred in Barbados and Zimbabwe, two of the three countries in which major near–term policy impact was achieved.

TRAINING

As noted above, one of the reasons for doing an assessment was to train local individuals in using the assessment model. USAID officials hoped to establish country–specific capacities for continuing use of the model for policy. In reality, the outside consultants who were versed in the use of the model did not have sufficient time to do much training in the typical application. Additionally, interest in learning about the model was low in many cases, since the local people had not been exposed to the model enough to pique their interest.

A meaningful amount of training was undertaken in only two countries.   In Costa Rica, a two–day training session was

conducted.   In Jordan, the   consultant worked directly with a group
of local officials for a month in completing the entire application
and sensitivity analyses.   In both cases, it is believed that local
officials are capable of using the needs assessment model on their
own as a result of the   training. Although the training appeared to
yield capable staff, the work had little effect in these particular
countries for larger reasons.   In the longer term, use of the model
by the people who were trained can be expected to have an effect as
the policy feedback begins.   All   countries will need their own
personnel to be trained if they are going to use the model on their
own. This has not happened   so   far because AID did not budget the
resources for it.

OVERALL ASSESSMENT

A review of the   questionnaires   comments about the overall utility
of using the housing needs assessment method yields some valuable
opinions. A sampling of quotations typifying these appears in
table 4.5.   The   striking   thing about these statements is
articulation of a facet of the   model to which, perhaps, not enough
attention has been paid: its   value   as   a device for organizing
discussions about housing policy and for stating clearly and
explicitly the magnitude of the problem facing the country.   If the
model succeeded only in this task, it would be viewed generally as
a worthwhile endeavor.

Perhaps the best advice is given by the last quotation in the
table: "Treat the needs assessment as one tool out of many; don't
give it undue weight; don't spend an excessive amount of time or
resources on it. Above all, know your local situation."

Table 4.5   OBSERVATIONS ON THE VALUE OF USING THE HOUSING NEEDS
ASSESSMENT MODEL

Costa Rica	The Housing Needs Assessment Method "removes the policy dialogue from one based on questionable feelings, personal bias to one predicated on a reasonably scientific basis."
Zimbabwe	"The exercise generated a number [housing needs] which was deemed rational and which gave an order of magnitude to the housing problem, thus permitting the problem to be discussed in proper perspective with other national needs, i.e., investment requirements, across all sectors of the economy."
Peru	It "removes some of the mythology of the 'housing deficit' concept. Most countries tend to overstate housing needs for political purposes."
Sri Lanka	"It puts you into the center of resource mobilization questions, which I believe is the high ground of influencing policy."
Jordan	It provided "a clearer idea of the potential relationships between factors affecting housing needs and investments. The base case for Jordan shows that [the country] can manage its housing situation with some modifications in its policies and programs."
Honduras	With the needs assessment, "policy discussion is based totally on numbers, not emotional responses and traditional ways of solving shelter problems."
El Salvador	"Treat needs assessment as one tool out of many; don't give it undue weight; don't spend an excessive amount of time or resources on it. Above all, know your local situation."

Note: These are quotations from completed questionnaires from the
survey of persons involved in applying the model.

Notes, chapter 4

1. Two questionnaires were developed—a longer one for the chief consultant, requesting more information on the level of effort and organization of the project, and a shorter one for all other respondents. Questionnaires were prepared in both English and Spanish. The longer questionnaire is included as appendix D. Brazil and the United States were not included because the applications had not been completed at the time of the survey.

APPENDICES

This appendix consists of two parts. The first describes the housing solutions used in the assessments: the physical standards used for dwelling upgrades, the minimum new unit, and the market rate unit for the base case. The descriptions are not strictly comparable because they depend on the information in the individual country reports. The second reviews the standards used to classify the base year housing stock into acceptable, upgradable, and nonupgradable categories. Rules for replacing housing stock are summarized in table A.1, costs of housing solutions in the base case in table A.2, household income levels and distribution in table A.3, and housing costs as a share of mean income in table A.4.

DESCRIPTION OF HOUSING SOLUTIONS, SELECTED COUNTRIES

Barbados

UPGRADE After upgrading, the unit has an indoor flush toilet and piped water; the unit rests on a permanent foundation and is free from any major structural deficiencies. Cost of an upgrade is $4,197.

MINIMUM NEW STANDARD The starter home is a 320 square foot dwelling consisting of a large, multipurpose room, kitchen, and full bath. It is of masonry construction with a concrete floor and minimum finishes. The unit is sited on a 3,000 square foot lot. The price of $12,000 includes the cost of the lot as well as the unit.

HIGHER STANDARD The basic unit is a 600 square foot, two bedroom, one bath unit. The floor area includes a covered patio. It is a

masonry unit with basic finishes on a 3,000 square foot lot.   The
cost of $16,240 includes both house and lot.

Botswana

UPGRADE The urban upgrade level is to provide sanitation (an REC2
latrine) to an existing unit, the cost of which includes the cost
of foundation, lining, slabwork, and structure.   Total cost is
$543.

MINIMUM NEW CONSTRUCTION The new unit is an 8 meter square, one-
room house with an REC2 latrine and water access. The total cost
includes Self-Help Housing Agency (SHHA) overhead and
infrastructure and land cost. Total cost is $1,687.

HIGHER STANDARD   The formal sector unit is a Botswana Housing
Corporation (BHC) L39-type unit.   It is a four-room house, 39
meters square. It has indoor plumbing and flush toilet. Total
cost is $10,626.

In the rural sector, the upgrade consists of providing
sanitation--a single pit latrine--to the existing unit. The total
cost of $283 includes foundation, lining, slabwork, and
construction costs.

The new unit is an SHHA type or modified SHHA-type with a single
pit latrine and water access.   The total cost of $1,230 includes a
one-room house, a single pit latrine, as well as overhead,
infrastructure, and land cost.

The formal sector unit is a BHC L39 type unit on a 39 meter
square lot. It is a four-room house with indoor plumbing and flush
toilet. The total cost of $10,478 includes building cost, BHC
overhead, and infrastructure and land cost.

Colombia

UPGRADE The upgrading loan plus value of existing minimal unit or
serviced plot with sanitary core cost $2,478.

MINIMUM NEW CONSTRUCTION   A 75   square meter serviced lot with core
unit. Cost is $4,055. The cost of the higher standard unit is set
at $7,593.

In the rural sector, the same standards are used and land costs
are assumed to be half as great.   The upgrading cost is $1,611;
while the cost of the second and third design level are $3,672 and
$7,029, respectively.

Ecuador

PRINCIPLE   These figures are based on estimates of housing
standards and costs as described in preliminary proposals being
considered by the Ministry of Housing.

UPGRADE   The upgrading program consists of supplying the
infrastructure such as water and sewer lines to each house;
electrical connection; street paving, sidewalks, and curbs; and
construction of a sanitary core for each house consisting of a
toilet, shower, and sink.   In metropolitan areas, costs were
computed for an 80 square meter lot. Total cost was $1,748 and was
assumed to be 10 percent less for other urban areas.

MINIMUM NEW CONSTRUCTION The second design level was based on a
lot size of 80 square meters.   Total cost of $10,166 includes the
cost of average land prices (substantially higher in the Sierra
region than in the coast region), infrastructure, house
construction (33 square meters), and indirect costs and
contingencies.

HIGHER STANDARD The unit occupies a 100-square-meter lot in metro
areas. The total cost of $18,299 incorporates all of the above
components except house construction, which is specified at 68
square meters.

In the rural sector, the upgrading would consist of providing a
sanitary water supply—either a well or water line where feasible—

an electrical connection, and either a septic tank or latrine for sanitary sewage disposal.   Rural upgrading would also include providing a sanitary core costing $1,021.

For the second level design, lot size in the rural sector was 300 square meters. Urbanized land cost less, bringing the total to $8,072. Cost of a higher standard unit in the rural area was $15,366.

El Salvador

UPGRADE The costs of upgrading include the value of materials needed to upgrade a 20 square meter house.   In addition to the loan, the affordability analysis takes into account the value of the existing dwelling being upgraded, which is the 1983 value of a typical tugurio unit, according to the 1976 Vivienda Popular study. The total cost is $1,160.

MINIMUM NEW CONSTRUCTION The serviced lot of 50 square meters has individual connections to the water supply and sewage systems, but with no structure of any kind.   Other services include surface drainage and compacted but unpaved streets.   Electricity is not included. The cost is estimated at $2,000.

HIGHER STANDARD The minimum basic house is a 24 square meter house with a 60 square meter lot of concrete posts and brick walls. All services, including electricity, are provided.   The cost is estimated at $5,960. For an additional $400, this solution could be provided with a concrete slab roof designed to permit construction of a second story.

In the rural sector, the construction costs reflect the use of local materials and "vernacular" construction methods (adobe or mud and wattle) to upgrade.

The basic 27 square meter unit consists of a soil cement floor, wooden columns, and a roof made of zinc sheets or clay tile. No wall are provided. The upgrade includes a pit latrine covered by a concrete slab, topped by a toilet seat, and sheltered by a roof. The total estimated cost is $640, which does not include land (in the rural areas, land is assumed already available to beneficiaries).

The minimum construction is the basic house with latrine or communal infrastructure package. This consists of a pit latrine shared by two families, and a water supply system with capacity for 50 families consisting of a well, a storage tank, a pump, and a pipe distribution system. The total estimated cost is $1,160.

Kenya

The report describes only the minimum new unit in urban areas. It consists of an 84 square meter cleared plot, water piped into the house, flush toilet and sanitary sewer, a 40 square meter unit with stone walls, cement floor, and corrugated iron roofing. Cost is $6,558. Upgrade and full new unit cost $1,123 and $8,969, respectively.

In rural areas, the costs of upgrades, the minimum new unit, and the full new unit are $326, $1,884, and $3,623, respectively.

Panama

UPGRADE Improvements in the housing stock can be achieved by new construction and through upgrading existing units, and would cost $2,752 in the metropolitan area and $2,400 in other urban areas.

MINIMUM NEW CONSTRUCTION The basic unit, termed by MIVI as vivienda basica adosada, sits on a 135 square meter lot that is provided with water and sewer services. Community streets and sidewalks are paved with gravel. The unit has exterior walls, roof, floor, and a sanitary unit consisting of a shower and toilet. Also included are a wash basin and a clothes washing area. The

total design area is 25.2 square meters.   The estimated cost in
1982 was $5,428 after adjusting for inflation.

HIGHER STANDARD The cost for a formal sector unit is $13,345 in
metropolitan areas and $11,643 in other urban areas.

In the country, the cost of an upgrade was estimated at $2,400:
a new unit was $4,740, and a standard formal unit was $11,640.

Peru

UPGRADE   The cost of upgrading is based on current Banco de
Materiales standards for upgrading a 40 square meter dwelling.   The
dwelling is assumed to be an informally built, incomplete house
constructed of brick or block.   The upgrading loan plus value of
upgradable informal unit is $1,978.

MINIMUM NEW CONSTRUCTION The serviced lots, estimated to be about
100 square meters in the Costa, 132 square meters in the Sierra,
and 180 square meters in the Selva, have individual connections to
water supply, sewerage, and electricity.   Other services include
surface and underground drainage and paved streets.   The estimated
cost is $4,795.

HIGHER STANDARD The minimum basic house is a 40–square–meter unit
built of brick, block, or both, but without finishes (acabados),
and stands on a serviced lot.   All basic accessories are provided,
including bathroom fixtures, doors, and windows.   The cost is
estimated at $11,949.

In the rural sector, the values of the loan and the unit to be
upgraded are estimated to be 30 percent lower than in urban areas.
The existing unit is assumed to be approximately 40 square meters
made of "traditional" materials (especially adobe), with no public
utility connections. The upgrading load plus value of upgradable
informal unit is estimated at $1,385.

MINIMUM NEW CONSTRUCTION   This design level has a communal infrastructure package which consists of a pit latrine shared by two families, a utility sink shared by two families, and a community water supply system consisting of a well, storage tank, pump, and pipe distributing system. Total cost is $1,053.

Sri Lanka

UPGRADE   Upgrading can occur on any of the components of an existing unit--cement floor, permanent roof, provision of water from a public standpipe, and public toilet. The cost is $360 in urban areas.

MINIMUM NEW CONSTRUCTION   A new unit is a shell house of 300 square feet, with a cement floor, roof on columns (no walls), laterite pathway, water from a public standpipe, and public toilet. The cost is $1,160.

HIGHER STANDARD   A completed house of 430 square feet consists of a hall, two bedrooms, kitchen, laterite street, individual water connection, and water-sealed toilet with septic tank, all costing $1,800.

In the rural sector, cost of an upgrade is $200; a minimum unit and a higher standard unit cost $1,040 and $1,600 respectively.

Zimbabwe

The minimum unit in urban areas is a 50 square meter unit on a 300 square meter plot. These are single-story detached units made of burnt brick, cement, or concrete block. Floors are concrete and the roof is of permanent material. Unit includes full bathroom with piped water running into the house. Cost is $5,883. Costs of upgrade and full new unit are $1,467 and $19,800, respectively.

The standards for rural areas are not described explicitly. The cost of an upgrade unit and market rate modest unit are $192 and

$19,800, respectively. The emphasis in rural areas is on upgrading the minimum new solution and is not defined separately.

DEFINITIONS CITED IN CLASSIFICATION OF THE BASE YEAR HOUSING STOCK

Barbados
PRINCIPLE The primary indicators employed in disaggregating the housing stock into various housing quality categories were the materials out of which the unit is constructed (wood, masonry, or mixed) and the presence of key amenities, particularly an indoor flush toilet (which implies the presence of piped water into the unit).
ACCEPTABLE A unit with an indoor W.C., a permanent foundation, and no major structural deficiencies.
NONUPGRADABLE Too dilapidated to restore economically.
UPGRADABLE All units between the other standards.

Botswana
PRINCIPLE Sanitation was the primary criterion for classifying base year stock.   A unit without access to communal facilities, flush toilet, or pit latrine was considered to be substandard.
ACCEPTABLE Any existing unit that meets the minimum sanitation requirements.
NONUPGRADABLE Squatter settlements (in the urban and primary growth areas) estimated to be less expensive to rebuild than to upgrade.
UPGRADABLE All units between the other standards.

Colombia
PRINCIPLE Strength of the material out of which the unit was constructed was the only criterion employed. The same definitions are used for urban and rural areas.

ACCEPTABLE   Units with   floor,   roof,   and walls all constructed of permanent materials.

NONUPGRADABLE   Units made wholly from impermanent materials.

Ecuador

PRINCIPLE   Housing stock   in   all   sectors   was   defined   by   a combination of criteria   based   upon   the   availability of sanitary toilet facility for the dwelling   unit and type of construction and construction materials applied.

ACCEPTABLE   Units which   satisfied   both criteria and classified as permanent.   For metropolitan and   other urban areas, dwelling units of certain construction   types—casa   or villa, apartment, boarding house,   and   mediagua   were   considered   as   satisfying   minimum acceptable construction materials standards.   In the rural sector, these construction type, plus rancho or coracha, were considered as satisfying the minimum   acceptable construction materials standard. In the rural sector, units   with   either exclusive or common use of standard toilet   facilities   or   sanitary   latrines were considered acceptable.

NONUPGRADABLE   Units that did not meet any of the above criteria.

UPGRADABLE   Units   of   permanent   construction that lacked sanitary toilet facilities and other   basic   services.   In metropolitan and other urban areas, units with   latrines were not considered to have met minimum   acceptable   standards;   in   rural   areas, nonpermanent units were considered   upgradable   primarily   by supplying sanitary toilet facilities.

El Salvador

PRINCIPLE   The categorization of   the housing stock was created and applied by MIPLAN   (the   Ministry   of   Planning and Coordination of Social and Economic Development), based   on the results of the 1978 Multi-Purpose Household Survey.

ACCEPTABLE Permanent and acceptable dwellings built primarily of masonry.

NONUPGRADABLE Dwellings built out of mud and wattle and discarded materials.

UPGRADABLE Dwellings built out of adobe, bahareque, or wood.

Kenya

PRINCIPLE No comprehensive, up–to–date, and fully reliable figures on the quantity and condition of the housing stock were available in Kenya.   Therefore, stock classification relied heavily on extrapolations from surveys made in specific localities.

ACCEPTABLE Units with access to safe drinking water and sanitary facilities.

NONUPGRADABLE Units lacking basic water and sanitary facilities, or poorly built, or with excessive densities.   Considered nonupgradable if no provision of infrastructure.

UPGRADABLE Substandard units with access to safe drinking water and sanitary facilities.

Panama

PRINCIPLE Units were classified following the MIVI (Ministry of Housing) standard described in the Census of Housing.

ACCEPTABLE Units classified by the Census of Housing as permanente and apartamiento.

NONUPGRADABLE (Vivienda improvisada) Dwellings made of wood and metal scraps, cardboard, or other temporary materials, located principally in Barriadas de Emergencia.   In the metropolitan area, the casa de vecinidad were principally modern tenements originally built as temporary housing to accommodate canal construction workers but still in service 70 years later.

UPGRADABLE Semipermanent units and physically satisfactory, but overcrowded.

Peru

PRINCIPLE The definitions of the housing stock categories rested
on a combination of structural characteristics and service
provision levels for housing units. 1981 Census figures on housing
quality and services were used.

ACCEPTABLE   Units considered permanent based on the extent of
permanent materials and the presence of water supply and sanitation
services

NONUPGRADABLE   Units constructed of temporary or improvised
materials (for example, quincha and reed mats).

UPGRADABLE   All units between   the two standards and units
constructed of permanent materials but lacking adequate water or
sanitation.

Sri Lanka

PRINCIPLE The critical unit features for which census data were
compiled were the strength of the roofing materials, source of
drinking water, and sanitary facility.   Two additional critical
considerations, but not measured by the Census, were adequate
ventilation and floor above a water seepage level.

ACCEPTABLE For all sectors--urban, rural, and estate--units made
out of permanent and semipermanent materials.   In addition, units
in urban areas must have piped water on or off premises; in rural
areas, piped water on or off premises or protected wells. Units
must also have water-sealed toilet in urban areas or pit laterine
in rural areas.

NONUPGRADABLE Improvised structures.

UPGRADABLE No specific government definition of upgradable units.
However, units that pass the above mentioned requirements for
acceptable units but have roofs made of palmyrah, cadjan, straw, or
similar material are considered upgradable, as are otherwise

acceptable units lacking adequate water supply or sanitary facilities.

Zimbabwe

PRINCIPLE Urban and rural housing stock were assumed to be very different. Categorization of housing stock depended upon government policies, for example, no improvised housing in the urban housing stock because of past government policies against the development of squatter settlements.

ACCEPTABLE Units of sound construction with access to piped water or flush toilets.

NONUPGRADABLE Units not located properly with respect to the MCHN housing development scheme, regardless of whether there rural housing stock was constructed of modern materials or a combination of modern and traditional materials.

UPGRADABLE Detached and semidetached dwellings and mixed units having elements of both modern and traditional construction and salvageable features.

Table A.1   RULES FOR DEFINING THE HOUSING PROGRAM

Country	Replacement of nonupgradable dwellings (annual percentage)	Improvement of upgradable units (annual percentage)	Elimination of crowding deficit (annual percentage)	Dwellings replaced (percentage of housing stock)
Barbados	5	5	5	1
Botswana	20[a]	12[a]	0	2
Colombia	5	5	5	2
Ecuador	5	5	5	2[b]
El Salvador	20	5	0	2
Kenya	5	5	5	2
Panama	5	5	5	1.5[b]
Peru	5	5	0	2
Sri Lanka	5	5	5	2[c]
Zimbabwe[d]	3.33	3.33	3.33	2

Note: Covers the base case for countries included. For all countries, an additional dwelling is needed for each newly formed household.
a. Replacement takes place only during the first five years, at the rate of 20 percent a year.
b. In the rural sector, construction materials have a shorter life span; dwelling units decay and are replaced at the rate of 3 percent a year.
c. For rural areas, the rate is 2 percent a year.
d. Assumes a 30-year planning period.

Table A.2   COSTS OF HOUSING SOLUTIONS IN THE BASE CASE (U.S. dollars)

Country	Year	Metro areas			Rural areas		
		Minimum Upgrade[a]	Higher standard	standard	Minimum Upgrade[a]	Higher standard	standa
Barbados	1980	4,853	10,507	16,240	4,853	10,507	16,2
Botswana	1984	543	1,687	10,626	283	1,230	10,4
Colombia	1985	2,478	4,055	7,593	1,611	3,672	7,0
Ecuador	1984	1,748	10,166	18,299	1,022	8,070	15,3
El Salvador	1983	1,160	2,000	5,960	880	1,200	2,2
Kenya	1983	1,632	6,558	8,969	508	1,884	3,6
Panama	1982	4,980	5,428	13,345	4,340	4,740	11,6
Peru	1984	2,709	4,795	11,949	1,385	1,053	7,2
Sri Lanka	1983	560	1,160	1,800	340	1,040	1,6
Zimbabwe[c]	1984	3,027	5,883	19,800	3,262	3,262	19,8

a. Cost for upgrade includes value of existing unit.
b. No water supply or sanitation facilities are included. If the communal infrastructure package is added, the cost of the house with communal servic is $8,278.
c. Housing costs for the upgradable and minimum standard units in rural are are based on a more realistic assumption of affordability by the rural population than in the government's proposal.

Table A.3   HOUSEHOLD INCOME LEVELS AND DISTRIBUTIONS

Country	Mean household Income (thousand US dollars)[a]	Share of Income in				
		Lowest quintile	Second quintile	Third quintile	Fourth quintile	Highest quintile
Barbados	5.08	0.03	0.08	0.15	0.26	0.48
Botswana	1.95	0.03	0.06	0.10	0.17	0.64
Colombia	5.54	0.05	0.10	0.13	0.20	0.52
Ecuador	6.45	0.05	0.11	0.13	0.21	0.50
El Salvador	3.83	0.03	0.07	0.11	0.27	0.52
Kenya	1.53	0.05	0.09	0.14	0.22	0.50
Panama	7.45	0.02	0.06	0.11	0.20	0.60
Peru	5.74	0.05	0.09	0.14	0.21	0.51
Sri Lanka	0.79	0.07	0.10	0.15	0.21	0.48
Zimbabwe	2.42	0.05	0.08	0.12	0.19	0.56

Source: Country studies; International Monetary Fund, International
Financial Statisitics 1984.
a. Local currency converted to U.S. dollars using exchange rates for year
ended 31 December 1983.

Table A.4 HOUSING COSTS AS SHARE OF MEAN INCOME

Country	Urban Areas			Rural Areas		
	Minimum Upgrade	Higher standard	standard	Minimum Upgrade	Higher standard	standard
Barbados	0.82	1.77	2.74	0.82	1.77	2.74
Botswana	0.24	0.75	4.70	0.13	0.58	4.97
Colombia	0.36	0.59	1.11	0.57	1.30	2.51
Ecuador	0.16	0.91	1.64	0.23	1.80	3.42
El Salvador	0.18	0.31	0.92	0.27	0.51	0.94
Kenya	0.31	1.78	2.36	0.28	1.61	3.10
Panama	0.31	0.61	1.49	0.42	0.83	2.04
Peru	0.16	0.66	0.95	0.59	0.45	3.09
Sri Lanka	0.50	1.03	1.60	0.47	1.43	2.21
Zimbabwe	0.33	0.53	1.77	0.30	0.30	2.98

Appendix B TOTAL HOUSING NEEDS IN DEVELOPING COUNTRIES

For much of the same planning reasons that individual nations want
to know their overall housing needs, donor organizations and the
countries supporting them desire an idea of the total needs of
developing countries. This appendix presents some order of
magnitude estimates of these total needs, building on the results
of applying the housing needs model successfully to 14 countries.[1]
Specifically, we estimate the number of additional units of
acceptable quality (produced either through upgrades or new
construction) that are needed and the corresponding investment for
the years immediately ahead to carry out a long-term program that
fully meets these nations' housing needs. The "years immediately
ahead" roughly matches the fifth year of the planning period in the
needs assessments. Estimates are provided by region of the world
and for countries grouped by per capita income level. The balance
of this appendix outlines the approach used in making the
estimates and presents the results.

ESTIMATION APPROACH

The procedure employed was to estimate regression models in which
the dependent variables were:

● total number of housing units needed in the fifth year of the
plan period per 1,000 population,

● ratio of housing investment to GDP.

The selection of independent variables was based on two
criteria: variables used in prior analyses of the ratio of housing
investment to GDP were taken as a useful guide[2] and the variables

had to be among those whose values were readily available on a consistent basis for most developing countries (World Bank 1986). The models were to be estimated using data from the 14 completed studies. Once the models had been estimated, we planned to obtain estimates for other countries by substituting the values of the independent variables for them into the estimated models and making some additional computations to yield estimates of the total number of units (new and upgraded) needed and the corresponding investment bill.

This procedure proved to work reasonably well for the ratio of housing investment to GDP. Both national income per capita and population growth rate were found to be significant determinants of this ratio, as in earlier analyses.[3] Still, the model explains only about 40 percent of the variation in the ratio. The projections done with the model should therefore be viewed strictly as order of magnitude estimates.

For computing total required investment, we were able to proceed as planned. The analysis not successful in estimating a statistically significant model for either the total number of housing units needed or the number of new housing units needed, with the explanatory variables available.[4] To provide some estimate, we used the average number of units per thousand population for the 14 countries in our sample (mean 13.55). As discussed in chapter 3, the variance around the mean value is quite small, suggesting that this simple approach should work reasonably well in the aggregate.[5]

RESULTS

The results of these calculations are shown in table B.1. These figures report the annual housing needs for all of the low- and middle-income countries listed in the World Development Report for which the necessary data are available.[6] According to these estimates, 44.2 million additional units meeting minimum physical standards will be needed annually in the years ahead; total cost will be about $130 billion.[7] The cost represents about 5.8 percent of the GDP of these countries on average—an apparently achievable overall goal, although the faster growing, lower income countries, in particular, will have to devote a larger share of national resources to housing to achieve this goal. Also, the volume of units needed is breathtakingly large compared to rough estimates of the level of minimally adequate units now being produced.

The lion's share in the number of new and upgraded units is needed in the low-income countries. Together, these countries account for two-thirds of the units needed (and a proportional share of the population). However, because of the cheaper solutions used by such countries, they would need a smaller share of total investment; our figure suggests only about 20 percent of the total.

Among the various regions Asia, with its enormous population, accounts for the majority of all units needed and about one-third of the total annual investment. In contrast, the Latin America region accounts for only 11 percent of the units required, but 38 percent of investment (owing to the higher building standards generally adopted and higher levels of national income devoted to housing).

Viewed from any angle, these figures indicate a staggering challenge to the countries themselves and to the donor community in mobilizing and employing the resources to produce the required units at minimum cost per unit.

Notes, appendix B

1. As indicated in the text, applications were attempted with 17 countries. One of these, Jamaica, was not completed successfully. Two, the United States and Brazil, were not completed at the time of the survey.

2. Key studies in this literature are those by Burns and Grebler (1977) and Buckley and Madhusudan (1984). Independent variables in the Burns-Grebler analysis included per capita GNP, the degree of urbanization, and population growth rates. The later analysis adds financial variables that could not be assembled for the large number of countries desired for inclusion in the projections. Other notable studies on the same broad topic include Renaud (1980) and Annez and Wheaton (1984).

3. The estimated model was:

HI/GDP = .898 + .00113 GNP/cap + 1.33 population growth rate
        (.48)   (1.48)   (2.79)

where HI/GDP = housing investment/GDP ratio
GNP/cap = GNP per capita

   $R2 = 0.42$ F = 3.91

The statistics appear in parentheses. The model and coefficients are significant at standard levels, using single-tailed tests.

   Some comment is in order on the parallels between past analysis of the HI/GDP ratio and this work. First, the dependent variable in this analysis is what investment will have to be to meet housing needs, not what it actually has been. Second, the variation among countries in standards adopted for the housing needs assessment presumably has some effect on the ratio. Third, it is likely that the data on ratio of actual housing investment to GDP in prior analyses contained a great deal of error in the housing investment figures; such errors may systematically decrease as income levels and levels of urbanization increase.

   Lastly, it might be noted that estimation of the model was complicated by very high linear dependency among the urbanization variable, GNP per capita, and population growth.

4. Annez and Wheaton (1984) have found that the number of new units constructed (relative to population) is largely independent of a country's income level but varies proportionately with population increase.

5. The coefficient of variation (the standard deviation divided by the mean times 100), a standard measure of relative dispersion, is 12.5 for this variable.

6. The necessary data were available for countries accounting for 3.53 billion people; countries excluded because of insufficient data had a combined population of 204 million. Two high-income countries, Oman and Libya, are included in the estimates; the estimates for other high-income countries were clearly unreasonable, presumably owing to the fact that the sample of countries used in the regression model included no countries in this income group.

7. It is difficult to judge the reasonableness of these figures, since few other estimates of this type have been attempted. One important set of estimates was made by the United Nations (1967) of the number of units needed each year in all the countries of Asia, Africa, and Latin America. While very crude comparisons suggest reasonable comparability between these estimates and this one, after allowing for differences in the time period covered (and, hence the larger base year populations used here), there are two types of important differences between the estimates. One is that the countries included have some important differences; the UN study included essentially all countries regardless of income level (for example, Japan), whereas ours is limited to developing countries for which data were reported in the World Development Report. Second, there are several important differences in the assumptions underlying the estimates; for example, the UN estimates assume much higher rates of unit obsolescence than those used in the Housing Needs Assessments. The UN assumes that the backlog at the beginning of the period is eliminated at a rate of 3.3 percent per year while the Needs Assessments typically use a 5.0 percent per year rate.

    Churchill (1980) reports another set of estimates of investment requirements. These are of the annual and total investment needed to provide minimally adequate housing to all households living in poverty in the year 2020, where the minimum unit is defined to be that affordable by a household at the poverty threshold. These estimates are not comparable with those presented here.

Table B.1 ESTIMATES OF ANNUAL CURRENT HOUSING NEEDS, DEVELOPING COUNTRIES

	Total units[a] (thousands)	Investment (billion dollars)
All countries[b]	44,775	130.6
Income group		
Low	30,310	24.0
Middle-low	8,452	26.8
Middle-high	6,013	73.4
Region		
East Africa	3,029	8.5
West Africa	2,378	5.9
East Asia-Pacific	18,184	30.2
South Asia	13,346	11.0
Middle East[c]	2,906	26.9
Latin America and Caribbean	4,992	48.1

Source: World Bank (1986)
a. Includes new and upgraded units.
b. See table B.2 for list of countries included.
c. Includes Oman and Libya (high income countries).

Table B.2 COUNTRIES INCLUDED IN ESTIMATES OF TOTAL HOUSING NEEDS, DEVELOPING COUNTRIES

Ethiopia	Madagascar	Zimbabwe	Syria, AR
Bangladesh	Ghana	Morocco	Malaysia
Mali	Sierra Leone	Papua N.G.	Chile
Nepal	Sri lanka	Philippines	Brazil
Zaire	Kenya	Nigeria	Republic
Burkina Fasso	Pakistan	Thailand	of Korea
Burma	Sudan	Cameroon	Argentina
Malawi	Senegal	Nicaragua	Panama
Uganda	Lesotho	Costa Rica	Portugal
Burundi	Liberia	Peru	Mexico
Tanzania	Mauritania	Guatemala	Algeria
Somalia	Bolivia	Congo	Uruguay
India	Yemen, PDR	Turkey	South Africa
Rwanda	Yemen, AR	Tunisia	Yugoslavia
Togo	Indonesia	Jamaica	Venezuela
Central Africa	Zambia	Dominican Republic	Greece
Republic	Honduras	Paraguay	Israel
Benin	Egypt, AR	Ecuador	Hong Kong
Guinea	El Salvador	Colombia	Singapore
Haiti	Ivory Coast	Jordan	Trinidad &
			Tobago
China			Oman
			Libya

Appendix C FURTHER DESCRIPTION OF THE HOUSING NEEDS MODEL

This appendix provides a more comprehensive, detailed description of the Housing Needs Assessment Methods. It summarizes the method in four steps: a listing of key attributes of the model and a sketch of the logic of the calculations involved; the results produced by the model; highlights of several critical assumptions undergirding the calculations that must be understood to interpret the results properly; and an outline of the computer hardware requirements and the extensive documentation available for the model.

KEY ATTRIBUTES

The computer model is essentially an accounting model as opposed to a structural equations or other econometric model. The model does, however, embody some behavioral assumptions that are highlighted in the third section of this appendix.

The analyst defines a plan governing the rate at which housing deficits present at the start of the period can be eliminated over the planning period. The deficits include units failing the minimum standards that must be replaced and those that can be economically upgraded; households living in overcrowded conditions are also included in the deficit. Additional sources of housing needs to be met annually are newly forming households and replacements for units leaving the housing stock.

The model normally employs a 20-year planning period. Results are produced for each fifth year in the period. These results are only for that year (not cumulative five-year totals), revealing the requirements for the number of units needed that year and the related investment requirements. While the model has a 20-year time horizon, the analyst can choose to eliminate base year housing deficits over a shorter or longer period; 20 years is simply the time dimension built into the model.

The model can also be run for a 5-year planning period, with suitable adjustments to the data inputs. Analyzing this shorter period, within the 20-year context, has proven especially useful in preparing programmatic documents such as 5-year plans.

MAJOR DISAGGREGATIONS

Several disaggregations of data in the model are important to understanding its capabilities.

First, a nation can be divided into as many as three housing sectors. The typical application has used the breakdown of major metropolitan areas, other urban areas, and rural areas. In Sri Lanka, the breakdown was urban, rural, and estate sectors. In some countries (for example, Barbados), the breakdown was only urban and rural.

Second, as part of the investment calculations, the model determines the value of housing that households can afford, or effective demand, based on their incomes, the share of their incomes available for housing investment, and the terms used to capitalize their investment. These affordability calculations are carried out by income quintiles for each housing sector.

Third, the model uses input data on the income distribution and average income by housing sector along with anticipated real growth in GDP to determine average household incomes by income quintile and sector for each year.

Fourth, in determining the quality of housing—both the structure and the associated infrastructure—that households can afford, the model includes three building standards for each

housing area: the   minimum   quality   upgraded   unit, the minimum
quality new   unit,   and   the   low-cost   market-produced   full unit.
Although each of these standards is based on a physical description
of the unit, the input   for   the   model   is   simply the cost of the
solution.

Fifth, the target group   is   defined   as households that cannot
afford the low-cost unit being offered in the market.

Sixth, based on   effective   demand   (affordability) and building
standards, the model computes total housing investment necessary to
meet the   housing   needs   by   sector   and   divides   it between what
households can   afford   by   themselves   and   the   subsidy needed to
permit target group households to occupy minimum quality units.

OPERATION OF THE MODEL

We can now give a rough outline   of the way the model operates (see
figure C.1).   The   major   determinants   of projected physical needs
for   shelter   are   future   population   growth,   household formation
trends, and adequacy of existing housing stock to meet the needs of
the current population.   As   shown   in figure C.1, these estimates
and projections are developed through modules 1 and 2 of the model.
Together, these determine the   scale   of   the housing program to be
analyzed through subsequent calculations.

The affordability of alternative   housing packages is determined
by current and   projected   incomes   of   the   various sectors of the
population and by the costs   of these alternatives.   These elements
of a housing needs assessment   are   considered   in modules 3, 4, 5,
and 6 of the model in the following manner:

● Module   3   projects   household   incomes   for   subsectors   of the
population by income distribution subgroupings.

● Module 4 calculates   housing   affordability for subsectors of the
population   based   on   household   incomes,   housing   expenditure
patterns, and terms of housing finance.

● Module 5 specifies the current and future costs of alternative shelter solutions defined on the basis of the dwelling standards established by planners.

● Module 6 classifies all households according to the housing standards they can afford.

On the basis of total shelter needs and the housing standards that are affordable by various segments of the population, modules 7 and 8 are used to:

● determine national housing investment requirements

● identify the target group for housing programs, based on inability to afford currently available, minimum standard, formal-sector housing.

● estimate any direct subsidy that might be needed to bring all housing to the chosen standard.

The information provided through these last two modules enables planners to evaluate the implications of alternative housing programs in relation to macroeconomic projections of investment and savings, public sector expenditures, formal sector loan volume, and other indicators.

RESULTS OF THE COMPUTATIONS

We focus here on the two primary outputs of the calculations: the number of units to be constructed and upgraded over the plan period and the corresponding levels of investment. The results from the application to Sri Lanka (Manson and Struyk 1984) are used for this illustration.

Table C.1 displays an output table reporting physical housing needs for urban areas. The "bottom line" of these computations is contained in the last two rows of figures, which show (in thousands) the number of new dwellings required at each fifth year in the plan period and the total number of acceptable units required (new plus upgraded units).

Some orientation for reading the rest of this table may be in order. For the base year of 1983, only data on the housing stock are presented. Except for the number of overcrowded units, which the model calculates internally, all these stock figures are input data supplied by the analyst. The figures for 1988 through 2003 are outputs; each column presents data only for the year at the head of the column. To obtain the total figures, the model deals with five different sources of housing needs listed in the left-hand stub of the table:

● Acceptable construction and replacements covers losses from the stock of acceptable units due to depreciation and other causes, for example, natural disasters. In this case, it was estimated that such withdrawals were equivalent to about 2 percent of the stock. In 1988, then, 4,690 new units (213,000 * .02) are needed for replacements.[1]

● Replacing nonupgradable units covers base year housing stock that is too deficient to warrant upgrading and must be replaced. The analyst determines, as part of the overall plan, the rate at which these units will be replaced. In this case the annual rate was assumed to be 5 percent, 2,400 replacement units a year (48,000 * .05).

● Upgrading existing units covers stock that is unacceptable in the base year but which could be made acceptable by improving the unit or the infrastructure services provided to it. The analyst determines the reduction rate for the backlog, in the case of Sri Lanka 5 percent a year. Some 13,300 units are thus scheduled for upgrading (267,000 * .05) in 1988.

● Overcrowding in 1983 is eliminated by 2003 in table C.2, at a rate of 5 percent per year, equivalent to 3,800 units (76,620 * .05). To relieve doubling up present in the base year, new units are scheduled for development.

● New households assumes that an additional dwelling unit is needed for every new household (the number of new households in each sector was computed earlier).

In summary, two key elements determine the level of housing needs in each year:

● the number of newly forming households, depreciation of acceptable units, and the extent of initial deficits

● the plan developed by the analyst for dealing with the deficits. The deficits can be scheduled to be eliminated in less than 20 years or not at all, depending on a country's policies, goals, and resources. In Sri Lanka, some 24,040 new units would be required in 1988 to meet the needs of new households, relieve overcrowding, and replace obsolete acceptable units and nonupgradable units. In addition, some 13,300 units would be upgraded. Hence, a total of 37,340 units are scheduled for some sort of activity in 1988. A central assumption of all calculations in the model is that the plan for each year is successfully accomplished.

Table C.2 presents the output table reporting the investment required to carry out the program of housing construction developed above. The total housing investment figure at the bottom of the table is the total cost required to meet the housing needs as specified in the plan. It includes the investments made by the "scheduled" households in the target and nontarget groups. For the latter group, who cannot afford the minimum solutions currently being marketed privately, it also includes the subsidy required for them to obtain an acceptable unit. The total investment is sensitive to the building design assumptions and, therefore, the costs for the various alternatives. The size of the target group is especially sensitive to the building standards employed.[2]

Total housing needs—that is, the sum of households or units scheduled for activity—are divided between the target and nontarget groups as follows: newly forming households and withdrawal of units from the existing stock are assumed to be distributed proportionately between the two groups; the needs for upgrading existing units, replacing nonupgradable units, and relieving overcrowding are assumed to be concentrated exclusively among the target population.

Investment by the nontarget group is based strictly on the affordability calculations. Investment by the target group has two components. The first is their own affordability: the calculations assume that these households invest the amount they can afford and therefore households that can afford to invest in housing do not stop investing when they obtain the minimum solution. Generally, some groups of households (defined by income quintile and sector) will not be able to afford the minimum solution assigned to them under the rules followed by the model in matching new and upgraded units to household groups.[3] In this case, the model computes the shortfall between what the households can afford with their own resources and the cost of the minimum solution to which they are assigned. The second investment component is the aggregation of these shortfalls, shown as "subsidy required" in the table. The subsidy is computed as a one-time grant required to make a unit affordable, although governments may well disburse subsidies in other forms. It is essential to note that the shortfall need not be closed entirely with subsidies, if households could be induced to use more of their own resources.

Investment levels depend critically on several key factors: the rate of growth of households, the size of initial housing deficits, income levels, income growth, the share of income available for housing investment, capitalization terms, and building standards selected.

Table C.3 illustrates the use of the model to analyze the impact of the policy changes or a range of values for data inputs. The table reproduces the result of a sensitivity analysis done for Sri Lanka, in which the applicable interest rate in the affordability calculations was increased from 8 percent to 12 percent. (Because only interest rates were changed, the numbers of new and upgraded units are unchanged.) The base case uses the 8 percent rate and

"ALT 1" uses 12 percent.   Since affordability declines as interest rates increase, total investment declines and the number of households needing subsidies and subsidy levels rise sharply. Similar analysis involving the factors listed above generally produce very informative results.

KEY ASSUMPTIONS

The foregoing discussion has glossed over some key assumptions underlying the calculations.   Understanding these assumptions is essential to interpreting the model's output properly and to assessing the utility of the overall method.   This section highlights and explains four particularly important assumptions.

Capitalization

The first concerns capitalization of monthly income available for housing investment. The ready analogy is to a household obtaining a mortgage loan, with the capitalization (the total investment figure shown in table C.2) representing the value of the housing purchased based on the mortgage payments (the "mortgage interpretation"). Unfortunately, the analogy has limited practical applicability in most developing countries, where the availability of mortgage financing from formal institutions is restricted to perhaps 20 percent of units built annually.

An alternative analogy is to incremental housing construction. Here the capitalized value gives the value today of a household monthly investment program equivalent to a mortgage payment (the "incremental investment interpretation).[4]

The same capitalized values can be reached via either route, but the difference in policy implications of these interpretations is critical. Under the mortgage interpretation, households obtain a unit of this value in the year in which they are scheduled under the plan to obtain it. Under the incremental investment interpretation, in contrast, the household willingly obtains its assigned solution 15 or 20 years in the future.[5] This is an important distinction, obviously, when explaining the model results to someone focusing on short-term improvement of housing stock.

Aggregate Subsidy

A second assumption concerns the estimate of the aggregate amount of subsidy required. In brief, this estimate embodies assumptions of almost perfect targeting of subsidy expenditures. Specifically, only those households that cannot afford a minimum unit receive a subsidy. In addition, the amount of the subsidy is limited to the difference between what a household can afford and the cost of the minimum unit. Finally, households are assumed to invest as much in housing as they would have without subsidies. Some of the rules allocating households "scheduled" for housing units to housing solutions offset the severity of these assumptions to some degree, but considerable target efficiency is nevertheless implied.

Housing Supply

We have not yet addressed housing supply. In fact, the model assumes that the necessary supply of new and upgraded units will be forthcoming each year at the prices in effect at the start of the year: an infinitely elastic supply curve. The price of housing is permitted to rise more or less rapidly than the overall price index. Thus, at the start of each simulation year the cost of each housing standard is adjusted for relative inflation in the housing sector. All other computations are in constant, base year prices. From year to year the supply curve can shift up or down, although it is horizontal within each year. Thus, an upward sloping supply curve over several years could reflect, for example, price increases expected as a result of sharp increases in the number of units produced annually. The analyst must specify any such anticipated inflation patterns.

The assumption that the plan-specified goals are accomplished each year can be avoided by running the model in five-year segments, adding to the deficits in each period to approximate the shortfalls experienced. This process is, however, awkward and time consuming. The model is designed to focus attention on the types of policy changes needed to address a country's housing needs fully over an extended period. Other simulation models exist for shorter term, more realistic policy analysis, but these are correspondingly more complex and data-intensive (Turner and Struyk 1985).

SPECIFICATIONS AND DOCUMENTATION

The computer program for this model is written in BASIC and operates in an MS.DOS environment on IBM, IBM-compatible, and Wang personal computers having at least a single disk drive and 128K of storage.[6] The program is fully "menu driven" and very easy to use. Data are entered into predefined table shells and multiple data files can be stored and retrieved. The model produces output tables (some of them several pages long) for each simulation. The output menu lets the user select only the tables he wishes to see. A separate "sensitivity analysis" routine compares key outputs from two or three simulations on a single page of output, which lets the user quickly determine the extent of changes associated with input data changes. There also are Spanish and French versions of the program.

The methods and the model proper are documented in substantial detail. Available documents fall into three groups. First is a general description of the overall method and the model, Preparing a National Housing Assessment (USAID 1984), available in English, Spanish, and French. Second is the Users Manual (USAID 1984a), available only in English. This explains how to use the computer model and provides greater detail on the functions employed in the model's calculations. It also provides table shells identical to those in the computer program for preparing data for input. The third form of documentation is the set of papers reporting the results of applying the method.   These are typically in English, but for a few Latin American countries they are in Spanish. These provide useful guidance on presentation and interpretation of calculation results. Reports for all the applications undertaken so far are included in the references.

An enhanced version of the model was developed recently. The principal improvements among the calculations concern the decay rates applied to permanent and upgradable units and the interest rates used in the affordability computations.   More substantial improvements have been made in the interactions between the user and the model, especially for reviewing output, which are incorporated into a new Users Manual (USAID 1986).

The various documents cited are available from USAID Document and Information Handling Facility; PPC/CDIE; SA-18, Room 209; USAID; Washington, DC 20523, U.S.A.

Notes, appendix c

1. In the "enhanced" version of the model, the development of which has just been completed, there are separate decay rates for permanent units and upgradable units.   These rates can differ for urban and rural areas, which is also the case in the original model.

2. Note, however, that it does not include investment made by households beyond that necessary to meet housing needs; so, for example, additional investment by higher income households who trade up by building larger units is not included.   For this reason, the total investment figure, as well as the share of GDP that would go to housing, is understated by some amount compared to what would actually be experiences if the plan were implemented.

3. To explain the allocation process a bit further, it began with
the point that the total number of new and upgraded units is
reached by calculating traditional housing needs. For households
in the target group in each sector, the number of units to be
upgraded first is allocated evenly among the income quintiles
making up the target group.   All remaining target group households
are allocated minimum new units.

4. In the enhanced version of the model referred to in note 1 of
this appendix, mortgage terms are permitted to vary by income class
as well as by sector.   This, in effect, permits the analyst to
differentiate between the cost of funds from formal and informal
sources. Experience in applying the model indicated that it is
important to take such cost differences into account if the
affordability calculations were to be accurate.   The new version
also can accommodate Graduated Payment Mortgages.

5. This capitalization procedure seems to overstate the amount of
investment that occurs in a particular year. The method assumes
that, in a steady-state environment, in which approximately the
same number of households begin their investment program each year,
the aggregate investment across all annual "cohorts" of investors
approximates the annual amount computed by the model.   This
assumption is less valid to the extent that large shifts in
population or household incomes are anticipated during the plan
period.

6. Wang PCs support more than one version of BASIC. The model will
work only with versions V1.03 and V1.04.

Table C.1 SRI LANKA BASE CASE: HOUSING STOCK AND HOUSING NEEDS,
URBAN AREAS (in thousand units)

	Actual	Annual projections			
	1983	1988	1993	1998	2003
Dwelling and construction standard					
Acceptable construction	213.00	376.26	541.22	704.38	864.06
(annual planned replacement)	(0.00)	(4.69)	(8.28)	(11.91)	(15.50)
Nonupgradable construction	48.00	36.00	24.00	12.00	0.00
(annual planned replacement)	(0.00)	(2.40)	(2.40)	(2.40)	(2.40)
Upgradable construction	267.00	200.50	134.00	67.50	1.00
(annual planned upgrading)	(0.00)	(13.30)	(13.30)	(13.30)	(13.30)
Total dwelling units	528.00	612.76	699.22	783.88	865.06
Overcrowded units	76.62	57.62	38.62	19.62	0.62
(annual planned construction)	(0.00)	(3.80)	(3.80)	(3.80)	(3.80)
New households per year	0.00	13.15	13.49	13.13	12.43
Construction of new units per year	0.00	24.04	27.97	31.24	34.13
Total construction per year	0.00	37.34	41.27	44.54	47.43

Table C.2   SRI LANKA BASE CASE: HOUSING INVESTMENT IN URBAN AREAS
(millions of rupees)

	1988	1993	1998	2003
Nontarget group investment	569.82	844.64	1,138.59	1,910.17
Target group investment	783.50	1,010.97	1,285.76	1,014.94
Subsidy required	214.95	255.27	288.83	332.68
Total housing investment	1,595.27	2,110.88	2,713.19	3,257.79

Note: Target group is defined as persons unable to afford a low-
cost unit available in the market.   Target group investment is all
the housing investment financed by the group's own resources.
Total housing investment for the target group includes both its
members' own investment and subsidies.

Table C.3   SENSITIVITY ANALYSIS EFFECT OF HIGHER INTEREST RATES, SRI LANKA

	1988			1993		
	BASE[a]	ALT 1[b]	ALT 2	BASE[a]	ALT 1[b]	ALT 2
Households needing subsidy (thousand units)						
Metropolitan areas	18.7	22.0	0.0	21.0	21.0	0.0
Other urban areas	72.4	88.9	0.0	89.1	105.6	0.0
Rural areas	7.5	9.0	0.0	8.4	9.9	0.0
Country	98.6	119.9	0.0	118.5	136.5	0.0
Percentage difference from base	0.0	21.6	0.0	0.0	15.2	0.0
Total housing investment (U.S. dollars)						
Metropolitan areas	1,595.3	1,329.2	0.0	2,110.9	1,753.0	0.0
Other urban areas	4,355.2	3,759.9	0.0	5,630.8	4,908.0	0.0
Rural areas	85.3	84.5	0.0	127.3	123.5	0.0
Country	6,035.89	5,173.6	0.0	7,869.0	6,784.5	0.0
Percentage difference from base	0.0	-14.3	0.0	0.0	-13.8	0.0
Subsidy requirement						
Metropolitan areas	215.0	296.6	0.0	255.3	359.4	0.0
Other urban areas	792.4	1,122.9	0.0	1,062.5	1,507.0	0.0
Rural areas	68.2	77.8	0.0	92.6	103.4	0.0
Country	1,075.6	1,497.3	0.0	1,410.4	1,969.8	0.0
Percentage difference from base	0.0	39.2	0.0	0.0	39.7	0.0

Note: In the Sri Lanka application, the geographic labels are somewhat
misleading.   Urban areas are labeled "metropolitan", rural areas "other urban,"
and the estate sector "rural."
a. An 8 percent interest rate was used in affordability calculations.
b. A 12 percent interest rate was used in affordability calculations.

Figure C.1   MAIN COMPONENTS OF THE HOUSING NEEDS ASSESSMENT MODEL

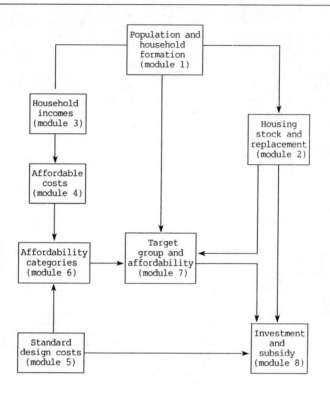

Appendix D HOUSING NEEDS ASSESSMENT

QUESTIONNAIRE FOR PRINCIPAL CONSULTANTS
(Please print or type all answers.)

Your name: _____

Firm, agency, etc.: _____

Title: _____

Country:[*] _____

Part A.

We begin with a few questions about how the assessment was carried out.

1. The presence of consultants in the field for a needs assessment has been organized in several different ways. Check which of the following best describes the organization in this case.

_____   1. The consultant(s) were present for a single visit of a few weeks.

_____   2. They were in-country for a data gathering visit, went back to their office and did much or all of the analysis, and then returned to discuss the findings.

_____   3. The consultants came for a visit and worked with host counterpart staff; they went away while the counterpart staff continued to work on the needs assessment; then the consultants returned and helped complete the assessment.

_____   Other: (specify)

2. What was the amount of elapsed time between when the consultant(s) first arrived and when the assessment was completed, i.e. the final report was completed?

_____   weeks.

----

* If you have participated in more than one housing needs assessment, please complete a separate form for each country.

2(a). What was the total level of effort by the consultants (in staff weeks) for this project?

_____ total, including preparation and work after returning from the field

_____ effort in the host country

3. In your case, how would you rate the amounts of time that the consultants had available to execute the project? (Check one)

_____ About right.

_____ Not enough.

_____ More than enough.

If you think there was too little, do you think it was because the total size of the effort was underestimated (for example, because data was more difficult to assemble than had been expected) or because more objectives were added to the original charge (for example, training) or other reasons. Please indicate the most important reason in your opinion.

4. There are several distinct tasks which are done as part of a needs
assessment. Here we would like to find out who had the lead
responsibility and who participated in each of several tasks. For each
task, place an "L" in the space if the person had the lead and "P" if
they participated; if you really don´t know anything about how a task
was done place "DK" in the space. (More than one L or P can be entered
for a single task where there was joint responsibility.)

<table>
<tr><td colspan="5">participant or lead</td><td>task</td></tr>
<tr><td>consult.</td><td>AID
Contr´tr</td><td>AID
offi´l</td><td>Gov´t
offi´l</td><td>Other</td><td></td></tr>
<tr><td>_____</td><td>_____</td><td>_____</td><td>_____</td><td>_____</td><td>1. data collection</td></tr>
<tr><td>_____</td><td>_____</td><td>_____</td><td>_____</td><td>_____</td><td>2. entering data in model/
running the model</td></tr>
<tr><td>_____</td><td>_____</td><td>_____</td><td>_____</td><td>_____</td><td>3. deciding on final data
values for base case</td></tr>
<tr><td>_____</td><td>_____</td><td>_____</td><td>_____</td><td>_____</td><td>4. interpreting results/
defining sensitivity
runs</td></tr>
<tr><td>_____</td><td>_____</td><td>_____</td><td>_____</td><td>_____</td><td>5. presenting results to
senior officials</td></tr>
</table>

5(a). Regarding the collection of the input data for use in the
computer model, were significant problems encountered? (Check one)

_____ Yes   _____ No

5(b). If the answer to the last question is yes, please name the area
in which real difficulty was encountered (for example, household size
data or income distribution) and then check the line that best
indicates the extent of the problem you had. (A list of data inputs is
attached at the end of the questionnaire for reference.)

Data Area	Extent of Problem			
	very difficult	almost difficult	impossible	adequate data never found
_____	_____	_____	_____	_____
_____	_____	_____	_____	_____
_____	_____	_____	_____	_____

5(c). How would you characterize the degree of cooperation you received in trying to assemble input data from government agencies and other individuals?

    _____ excellent.

    _____ very good in general, but with one or two exceptions.

    _____ generally pretty good, but one or two important problem areas.

    _____ fairly difficult overall.

    _____ other (specify).

6(a). Did the team doing the needs assessment make use of either a formal or informal advisory group? (Check one.)

    _____ Yes   _____ No

6(b). Who was primarily responsible for setting up the group? (Check one.)

    _____ consultant team

    _____ RHUDO or AID official

    _____ counterparts

    _____ other (specify) _____

6(c). If the team did have an advisory panel, please indicate the kind of institutions these people represented and their level in the organization (e.g., staff, senior management).

6(d). How helpful do you think the advisory group was? Would you
recommend use of such a group to other countries making a needs
assessment?

6(e). If you did not have an advisory group, how was advice solicited
above the input data, interpretation of the results, and decisions about
which sensitivity analyses to undertake?

7. Now, a couple of questions about how the results were presented at
the completion of the formal needs assessment. First, which of the
following describes the presentation of the results. (Check all that
apply.)

_____ The results were presented at a meeting attended by some
         senior officials, other government officials, private sector
         representatives, the project team and some AID staff. (Cross
         out any that do not apply.)

_____ There was an informal briefing of senior government
         officials.

_____ No briefings took place at this time. Later counterpart
         staff or AID contractors did some briefings.

_____ Other (specify)

7(a). As a result of these briefings were any revisions later made to
the analysis? Was additional analysis undertaken, either by counterpart
staff or by the consultants? Please briefly describe.

8. Finally, how well did the RHUDO and/or local PRE/H staff generally prepared the way for you visit before you arrived, in terms of explaining the purpose of your work to local government officials, setting up meetings, etc.?

_____	Excellent	_____	Some preparation was done
_____	Did a good job	_____	We were really on our own
_____	Other (specify)		

Part B.

This part concentrates on the purposes and impacts of having done a needs assessment.

9. In retrospect, at the time this work began who did you think was the primary audience for the housing needs assessment?

Who turned out to be the real audience? (Please rank the different audiences in order of importance; 1, 2 . . .)

initial   actual

_____   _____   AID staff, either in Washington or the RHUDO?

_____   _____   Local AID staff?

_____   _____   Policy makers or officials at the housing, planning or other ministries?

_____   _____   Other (specify) _____

10. Needs assessments have been undertaken for several reasons. Which of the following best describes your perception of the primary objectives in doing this assessment at the time the project began, and your perception at the end of the project. (Please rank the different reasons, in order of importance.)

initial final

_____ _____   performing a good technical assessment

_____ _____   training counterparts in the use of the
                methodology

_____ _____   developing a strong policy dialogue based on the
                results of the assessment

_____ _____   I had no firm understanding of the relative
                priorities of these various objectives

_____ _____   Other _____

11. Now a question about the technical quality of the needs application. At the time the project was supposed to be completed, which of the following best describes the situation.

11(a). The application was not completed because of data problems?

_____ Yes, not complete   _____ No, completed

11(b). If it was completed, which of the following best characterizes the product? (Check one)

_____   The application was satisfactorily completed and there were
        no diagreements among those involved about inputs or the
        various cases simulated.

_____   The application was completed and there was no significant
        disagreements about the calculations themselves, although
        there may have been disagreements about whether the correct
        building standards were selected or other "policy" issues

_____   The application was complete but there were serious
        reservations about the data inputs and/or the way in which
        the model did the calculations.

_____   Other _____

12. One objective of some applications was to provide training in the housing needs assessment methodology to counterpart and AID staff. Was any training in how to carry out a needs assessment done of AID staff (including in-country consultants) or counterpart staff as part of this needs assessment?

_____ Yes   _____ No   _____ Don´t know

12(a). Had anyone who was involved more than casually with the needs assessment already has some exposure or training in this particular methodology, for example at a MIT short-course or at a Habitat conference? If the answer is yes, please indicate the number of people in the yes block.

_____ Yes (number)   _____ No   _____ Don´t know

12(b). Often the only actual training that was done was for the consultants to make a presentation about how to use the methodology. This presentation was typically not part of the presentation of the results of this application and frequently it included a session at the computer to demonstrate the computer model. Was such a session done as part of the application in this country?

_____ Yes   _____ No   _____ Don´t know

12(c). If training went beyond the type of presentatioan just indicated, in which of the following activities, if any, did the "trainees" participate? (Mark all that apply)

	who participated	
	AID staff	counterparts
assembling the input data	_____	_____
running the model	_____	_____
reviewing the preliminary results	_____	_____
reviewing the final results	_____	_____
making presentations to higher officials	_____	_____
writing the report on the application	_____	_____

12(d). By the time the consultants completed their assignments, were there any host country personnel who were fully capable of using the model--both running the computer model and interpreting the results?

_____ Yes   _____ No   _____ Don´t know

12(e). To your knowledge, has any counterpart staff used the assessment methodology since the completion of the initial project?

_____ Yes   _____ No   _____ Don´t know

If the answer is yes, could you describe briefly the type of work that has been done and whether the analyst was able to complete it successfully?

12(f). Do you think that more training of the counterpart staff (possibly in addition to someone who already is competent with the model) is needed for them to be able to use the methodology on their own? Do you think that they really would welcome such training?

need training: _____ Yes   _____ No   _____ Don´t know

want training: _____ Yes   _____ No   _____ Don´t know

13. A primary objective in many of the housing needs assessments was to cause a reconsideration of the country´s housing policies in light of the total housing needs which the country must confront over the next 20 years.

13(a). Did the results of the needs assessment cause any serious discussion within government, or between government and funding agencies, about its policies?

_____ Yes   _____ No   _____ Don´t know

13(b). If the answer to the last question was "yes", can you recall what specific issues were discussed? Please summarize these below.

13(c). Were any actual policy changes determined as a result of this process? If so, please outline these below.

13(d). Have the results of the assessment been used in actual planning exercises like the five year plan? Have some of the results appeared in official planning documents?

used in planning _____ Yes _____ No _____ Don't know

appeared in documents _____ Yes _____ No _____ Don't know

Which documents?

13(e). Was a consultant (either part of the original team or someone else) invited to the country to do follow-up work on the needs assessment?

_____ Yes _____ No _____ Don't know

If the answer is yes, what were the primary reasons for this person being asked to work on the assessment? (Check all that apply.)

_____ Doing additional policy analysis

_____ Doing additional training with counterpart staff

_____ As part of another study

_____ To redo some of the initial anlaysis because of problems with the analysis or to exploit additional data

_____ Other _____

13(f). If the results of the housing needs assessment have not had any influence on policy discussions or planning, why do you think that has been? Please be as specific as possible.

14. In your own words, how would you rate the overall usefulness of the application of the needs assessment in this country and its impact on policy discussions? What factors do you think were most critical in determining these outcomes?

15. If a colleague in another country were about to undertake a needs assessment with AID's assistance, what key piece of advice would you give him about how to get the work out of this effort?

Table D.1 TABULATION OF RESPONDENTS TO SURVEY ON HOUSING NEEDS
ASSESSMENTS

Country	Consultants on project	Last country staff	AID personnel	Others[a]	Total
Barbados	1	1	--	1	3
Botswana	1	--	1	--	3
Colombia	1	--	--	--	1
Cost Rica	1	--	1	--	2
El Salvador	1	--	2	--	3
Ecuador	2	--	1	--	3
Honduras	1	--	1	--	2
Jamaica	--	--	--	1	1
Jordan	1	1	--	--	2
Kenya	1	1	--	--	2
Panama	2	1	1	--	4
Peru	1	--	1	--	2
Sri Lanka	2	--	1	--	3
Turkey	1	2	--	--	3
Zimbabwe	2	1	--	1	4

a. Includes others working under AID contract in the country.

Table D.2 HOUSING NEEDS ASSESSMENT MODEL INPUT DATA REQUIREMENTS

Variables	Year[a]	Regions[b]	Quintiles	Units
		Level of Disaggregation		
Population	all	MOUR		thousands
Household size	all	MOUR		units
GDP	base	country		millions
GDP real growth rate	future	country		percent
Rural share of GDP	all	country		percent
Average household income	base	MOUR		thousands
Household income distribution shares	all	MOUR	yes	percent
Upgrading cost	base	MOUR		thousands
Value of upgradable units	base	MOUR		thousands
New housing unit cost	base	MOUR		thousands
Current formal sector housing cost	base	MOUR		thousands
General inflation rate	all	country		percent
Construction cost escalation rate	all	country		percent
Upgradable units	base	MOUR		thousands
Non-upgradable units	base	MOUR		thousands
Acceptable units	base	MOUR		thousands
Annual upgradings	future	MOUR		thousands
Annual replacement of non-upgradable units	future	MOUR		thousands
Annual new units to relieve over-crowding	future	MOUR		Thousands
Acceptable housing decay rate	constant	MOUR		percent
Upgradable housing decay rate	constant	MOUR		percent
Mortgage interest rate (nominal)	constant	MOUR	yes	percent
Mortgage Loan Term	constant	MOUR	yes	years
Downpayment percentage	constant	MOUR	yes	percent

Table D.2 (continued)

Variables	Year[a]	Regions[b]	Quintiles	Units
	Level of Disaggregation			
Graduation rate (optional)	constant	MOUR	yes	percent
Graduation period (optional)	constant	MOUR	yes	years
Housing expenditures share of household income	constant	MOUR	yes	percent
Recurring expenditures share of housing expenditures	constant	MOUR	yes	percent
Public sector capital expenditures	base	country		millions
Total housing investment (formal and informal sectors)	base	country		millions
Share of land, infrastructure, and construction in housing costs	base	MOUR		percent

a. Base year only, future years only, all years, or assumed constant.
b. Metropolitan, other urban, and rural (MOUR), or total country only.
c. "Yes" if data must be provided for all five quintiles of the income distribution.

REFERENCES, GENERAL

Annez, P., and W. Wheaton.   1984.   "Economic Development and the
Housing Sector: A   Cross-Sectional   Model."   Economic
Development and Cultural Change, vol. 32, no. 4, pp. 249–66.

Buckley, R., and R.G. Madhusudan.   1984.   "The Macroeconimcs of
Housing's Role in the Economy: An Introductory Analysis."
Maxwell School Working Paper.   Syracuse University, Syracuse,
N.Y.

Burns, L.S., and L. Grebler.   1977.   The Housing of Nations.   New
York: Wiley and Sons.

Churchill, A.A. 1980.   Shelter.   Poverty and Basic Needs Series.
World Bank. Washington, D.C.

Keare, D., and S. Parris.   1982.   Evaluation of Shelter Programs
for the Urban Poor.   World Bank Staff Working Paper no. 547.
Washington, D.C.

Malpezzi, S., S. Mayo, and D. Gross.   1985. Housing Demand in
Developing Countries. World Bank Staff Working Paper no. 733.
Washington, D.C.

Mayo, S., with D. Gross.   1985.   "Sites and Services—and
Subsidies: The Economics of Low-Cost Housing in Developing
Countries." Washington, D.C.:   World Bank, Water Supply and
Urban Development Department.

Merrett, S. 1984.   "The   Assessment of Housing Consumption
Requirements in the Developing Countries."   Third World
Planning Review, vol. 6, no. 4, pp. 319–29.

Renaud, B. 1980.   "Resource Allocation to Housing Investment:
Comments and Further Results,"   Economic Development and
Cultural Change, vol. 28, no. 2, pp. 389–99.

Struyk, R. J. 1984.   AID Housing Needs Assessment Model: User's
Manual. Washington, D.C.: The Urban Institute.

Struyk, R., and M. Turner.   1986.   Finance and Housing Quality in
Two Developing Countries: Korea and the Philippines.
Washington, D.C.: The Urban Institute.

Turner, M., and R. Struyk.   1985.   The Housing Quality Simulation
Model: Basic Description. Washington, D.C.: Urban Institute
Report to USAID Office of Housing and Urban Programs.

United Nations. 1967. Methods of Estimating Housing Needs. U.N. Series F, no. 12. New York: Department of Economics and Social Affairs Studies in Methods.

United Nations. 1965. World Housing Conditions and Estimated Housing Requirements. Document ST/SOA/58. New York: Department of Economic and Social Affairs.

USAID, Office of Housing and Urban Programs. 1984. Preparing a National Housing Needs Assessment. Occasional Paper. Washington, D.C.

World Bank. 1986. World Development Report 1985. New York: Oxford University Press.

REFERENCES, COUNTRY STUDIES

Barbados   Dubinsky, R., and R. Struyk. 1985. Revised Estimates of Housing Needs and Investment in Barbados: 1980-2000. Urban Institute report to USAID Office of Housing and Urban Programs. Washington, D.C.

Botswana   Clifton, C.S., and A.D. Roscoe. 1984. Botswana: An Assessment of National Housing Needs, Affordability, and Potential Barriers to Successful Implementation. Robert R. Nathan Associates, Inc. Report to USAID Office of Housing and Urban Programs. Washington, D.C.

Colombia   Planning and Development Collaborative International. 1984. Columbia: Shelter Sector Assessment. Report to USAID Office of Housing and Urban Programs. Washington, D.C.

Costa Rica   Planning and Development Collaborative International 1986. Diagnostico y Pronostico de Necesidades de Vivienda en Costa Rica, 1985-2005. PADCO Report to USAID Office of Housing and Urban Programs. Washington, D.C.

El Salvador   Planning and Development Collaborative International. 1984. El Salvador: Shelter Sector Assessment. Report to USAID Office of Housing and Urban Programs. Washington, D.C.

Ecuador

Blankfeld, R., and S. Vergara. 1984. An Assessment of National Housing Needs and Affordability in Ecuador: 1984-2004. Robert R. Nathan Associates, Inc. Report to USAID Office of Housing and Urban Programs. Washington, D.C.

Honduras

Planning and Development Collaborative International. 1986. Diagnostico y Pronostico de Necesidades de Vivienda en Honduras: 1985-2005. PADCO Report to USAID Office of Housing and Urban Programs. Washington, D.C.

Jordan

Struyk, R., and Shelter Unit, Ministry of Planning. 1986. Housing Needs and Associated Investment in Jordan, 1985-2005: Preliminary Estimates. Amman: Ministry of Planning.

Kenya

Rourk, P., and A. Roscoe. 1984. An Assessment of National Housing Needs and Affordability in Kenya: 1983-2003. Robert R. Nathan Associates, Inc. Report to USAID Office of Housing and Urban Programs. Washington, D.C.

Panama

Peterson, G., et al. 1985. Urban Development Assessment: Panama. Robert R. Nathan Associates, Inc. and Urban Institute Report to USAID Office of Housing and Urban Programs. Washington, D.C.

Peru

Planning and Development Collaborative International. 1986. Peru: Shelter Sector Assessment. Report to USAID Office of Housing and Urban Programs. Washington, D.C.

Sri Lanka

Manson, D., and R. Struyk. 1984. Housing Needs and Probable Investment in Sri Lanka 1983-2003. Urban Institute Report to USAID Office of Housing and Urban Programs. Washington, D.C.

Turkey

Manson, D. 1985. Policy and Institutional Framework in Turkey, Vol. II: Housing Needs and Investment Requirements. Urban Institute and USL International Report to USAID Office of Housing and Urban Programs. Washington, D.C.

Zimbabwe   Manson, D., and H. Katsura.   1985. Housing
                    Needs Assessment   Study: Zimbabwe.   Urban
                    Institute Report to USAID Office of Housing and
                    Urban Programs.

Note: The assessments for Brazil and the United States were still
underway when this report went to press.   The assessment in Jamaica
was unsuccessful.